Between Breaths

A MEMOIR OF
PANIC AND ADDICTION

Elizabeth Vargas

GRAND CENTRAL
PUBLISHING

NEW YORK   BOSTON

Grand Central Publishing
Hachette Book Group
1290 Avenue of the Americas
New York, NY 10104
grandcentralpublishing.com
twitter.com/grandcentralpub

First edition: September 2016

Grand Central Publishing is a division of Hachette Book Group, Inc.
The Grand Central Publishing name and logo is a trademark of Hachette Book Group, Inc.

The publisher is not responsible for websites (or their content) that are not owned by the publisher.

Library of Congress Cataloging-in-Publication Data

Names: Vargas, Elizabeth, author.
Title: Between breaths : a memoir of panic and addiction / Elizabeth Vargas.
Description: New York : Grand Central Publishing, [2016]
Identifiers: LCCN 2016009767| ISBN 9781455559633 (hardback) | ISBN 9781455566037 (large print hardcover) | ISBN 9781478929932 (audiobook)
Subjects: LCSH: Vargas, Elizabeth—Health. | Alcoholics—Biography. | Television news anchors—United States—Biography. | BISAC: BIOGRAPHY & AUTOBIOGRAPHY / Personal Memoirs. | BIOGRAPHY & AUTOBIOGRAPHY / Rich & Famous.
Classification: LCC HV5275.V37 2016 | DDC 362.292092 [B]—dc23
LC record available at https://lccn.loc.gov/2016009767

Printed in the United States of America

LSC-C

10 9 8 7 6 5 4 3 2

For My Beautiful Boys,
Zachary and Sam

Author's Note

There are people who will say I have not been sober long enough to write this book, that I should wait until I have eight years without a drink, or eighteen.

Perhaps they are right. But there is not a magic number of years of sobriety that suddenly confers authority or expertise, or even a guarantee that it will last.

I am not an expert on alcoholism. I do not claim to know all the secrets to getting better, and as you will read, I have learned painful lessons about what is important. I just know what finally worked for me, and that my sobriety, while new, is hard won and my life is so much better for it.

I am not an expert on anxiety, either. But it has been a part of my life since I can remember. In 2013 the National Institute on Mental Health estimated 40 million American adults suffered from anxiety, and that number did not include the many children growing up in its grip, as I did. I am just one of many who struggle, one of the lucky few who finally found a way to not let it run my life. That, too, is a daily battle.

What I do for a living is tell stories...on television.

They can be big, sweeping tales of bravery and tragedy or smaller gems about kindness, perseverance, and quiet courage. I am always honored when people share their stories with me, when they trust me with their deepest fears and secrets.

This book is my story. It is personal and it is evolving. I don't have all the answers, and life didn't magically get better all of a sudden when I stopped drinking. My anxiety didn't vanish forever. But it is so much better than it was, and I am grateful to be able to tell the story of how I finally found a place of grace.

Introduction

Spring 2002—New York City

I'm sitting at the anchor desk in the large studio we call TV3, illuminated by more than two thousand watts of lights hanging above me, in front of me, even behind me. I'm tethered to the desk by a small microphone pinned to my dress; a tiny device in my ear, called an IFB, allowed the producers and director in the control room to speak to me. Four huge robotic television cameras point at me from different angles. It's 6:25—five minutes to air. I, along with the staff at ABC's *World News Tonight*, have worked together that whole day to prepare the live broadcast that is about to start. As a team, we have spent hours meticulously selecting the stories we would tell, those that were most important, or most searing, to be included in that night's show. But now, even though we have worked as a group, I feel very alone. It was up to me and me alone to deliver the scripts we'd carefully crafted, and I was freaking out.

The studio is frigid. I like it that way; it makes me anxious to feel too warm. I had only allowed myself to nibble on some pretzels and fruit all afternoon because it unnerves me to feel food in my stomach when I anchor a live show. I try deep yoga breathing to calm my hammering heart in my chest. I've taken half of a beta blocker to help with that. *Did I take enough? Why is my heart still beating so hard? If I take too much my mouth will get dry and I won't be able to talk. I think I feel queasy. Should I swig some Pepto-Bismol or is it too late for that to help?* I reach for the mug of hot water with lemon next to me. I grip it with both hands because I'm trembling. Could anyone in the control room looking at all those images of me through all those cameras see me shaking? The stage manager, Michelle, hollers, "One minute to air." The studio begins to swim slightly around the edges. "Thirty seconds!" she shouts. I take another tiny sip of water and another deep breath. "Ten, nine, eight, seven…" *Dammit, I really wish she wouldn't count down like that.* "…two, one, we're on the air."

The show's opener rolls: "This is *World News Tonight*, reported tonight by Elizabeth Vargas." I draw in a deep breath, grip the desk hard with my right hand, and press the sharp edge of my engagement ring into my left thumb. I need these physical reminders to stay focused, to stop worrying that I might vomit on live TV or have a panic attack and hyperventilate. I then look directly into the camera and say, "Good evening. We begin tonight…"—and thirty minutes later, it is done. I rarely stumble over the words in the script, and I am usually able to focus intensely on the stories in the newscast. Once I get past the first block, I can relax and, some nights, even enjoy this job I love so much. Afterward, we all troop down-stairs to the news rim; there, we sit at desks in a circle and discuss what worked, what didn't, what the competi-tion led with, and how the order of our stories compared. There is always, for me, a certain giddiness when it's over, and a sense of being wrung out from the effort it takes not just to manage my anxiety, but to conceal it.

And then an overwhelming feeling: *Dear God, I need a drink.*

PART I

Chasing the Glow

I don't know if I was born an alcoholic, but I was definitely born anxious. The alcoholism came to me later in life, after years of drinking to ease stress and worry, and to fend off panic. But the anxiety? It was there from the start. My earliest memories are infused with it. It was a steady theme throughout my childhood, and it is the background music of my adult life. Sometimes it was loud and intrusive; other times you could barely hear it. But it never left me. I dabbled in drinking in high school, didn't drink at all in college, and then after graduation drank moderately (or at least what I thought was moderately) for nearly two decades. But even from the start, in my early twenties, I liked alcohol. I liked the way it made me feel. There's a sweet feeling that you get from those first few glasses of wine. The world is softer, smoother, more golden; the tension drains from the tightly clenched muscles in my neck and shoulders. I could finally breathe. I would go out with my friends after work in local news. Everyone seemed smarter and prettier and more interesting, even me. We would toast our good fortune, celebrate the newscast we had just put on live TV, clink our glasses to another victory in the ferociously competitive business in which we all worked. The nervous worry and the edginess I carried with me all day would melt away, and I would bask in a chardonnay glow.

Some people chase that alcohol glow their whole life, and somehow they make it through, or they learn along the way that there are other, better ways to ease anxiety. I did not. Drinking started out to be something that felt lovely and luxurious. It was a romance of sorts. It ended with me on the brink of dying from alcohol poisoning, of losing every single thing and every single person I treasured. It sent me to a hardscrabble rehab in Tennessee, where I spent a grim Christmas alone, my two precious children nine hundred miles away, opening gifts without their mom. There is nothing remotely romantic about that.

My problem was that at some point, the alcohol stopped working. The more I chased that glow, the more elusive it became. Determined to rediscover it, I would drink more. One or two glasses a night became three or four. The relief I once enjoyed was now slipping from my greedy hands, leaving me with my anxiety tapping on the door. Drinking too much nearly always had consequences—simple hangovers at first, nothing a Gatorade and an hour at the gym couldn't fix. But the opening in the window between when alcohol made me feel better and when it extracted its heavy toll became narrower and narrower. The hangovers morphed from bleary, shaky mornings to entire days when I counted the hours until I could go home and have another glass of wine, so desperate I was for that relief. And it wasn't just anxiety I was looking to drown. It was fear. I was insecure and terrified someone would wake up and say "Hey, what are you doing here? You don't belong here!" and then unceremoniously show me the exit. That fear was there whether I was in a newsroom or at a dinner party, board meeting, or movie premiere. The world would see me for the fraud that some part of me had always believed I was. Deep down, I wasn't a confident, in-control network news anchor and the happily married mother of two wonderful children enjoying life in one of the most exciting cities in the world. Inside I was still a panicked five-year-old living in abject terror. I was living a double life, hiding the anxious, worried version of myself that spent her entire life poised at the starting line, every muscle tensed, straining to hear the sound of the shot that would send her sprinting in panic as if her life depended on it. I spent most of my life believing I was the only one who hid her secret self from the world, that everyone else was as perfect and happy as they seemed to be. I know better now. Everyone has something that scares them. Everyone must make a choice at some point whether to be brave. Everyone has a story. Mine begins with a frightened little girl...

—⚏—

There Was a Little Girl, Who Had a Little Curl, Right in the Middle of Her Forehead

My mother and father were young when I was born and, as they will be the first to tell you, relatively clueless about parenting. I was their first child, and I was a handful. I had colic, and I cried nonstop. It was the era of Dr. Spock, whose advice to mothers and fathers was received like Holy Scripture. If your baby cries, he counseled, leave her be; soon enough she'll cry herself to sleep.

My overwhelmed parents listened to Dr. Spock and left me in my crib to wail for hours, while they worried in the next room. By the time I was a year old I was soothing myself by rocking the crib, back and forth, for hours every night. There are many toddlers who do this. I did it until I was eight years old. It was the only way I knew to make myself feel better.

When I was four my father, who was a captain in the U.S. Army, received orders to move to Okinawa. It was in the middle of the huge troop buildup in the Vietnam War, nearly two thousand miles from my dad's new post. The base was crowded, and there were no houses available. Rather than leave my mother; my three-year-old brother, Chris; and me behind in the States, my dad looked for a home off base, "on the economy," as those in the military call it. That way, we could all stay together. We packed our bags and got our vaccines and boarded the long flight for Japan.

We arrived in November 1966 to an unseasonable chill and a steady rain. My dad scraped together $2,500 to buy a brand-new concrete and cinderblock house on a small street. That house turned out to be a catalogue of terrors and phobias for a young child. The concrete had not set when we moved in: it was cold and damp. My mother covered the floors of our closets and lined our drawers with tinfoil to keep the mildew out of our clothes and shoes. The steady, relentless rain turned the alleys around our house into streams and the fields into marshes. Our sodden little house didn't stand a chance. Water poured in everywhere. Our ceilings began dripping in dozens of places. We scattered all of our pots and pans around on the floor to catch the rainwater, plinking and plonking all over the house, a symphony of waterworks.

We didn't have a telephone, so we went to our neighbor's to call the Japanese man who had built the house.

"It's raining in the house!" my mother wailed.

That proved to be too long a sentence for the builder's few words of English.

"Rain, yes," he said, in a tone that implied that it was

unremarkable for there to be rain. Clearly the idea that water was coming into the house had not made it across the language barrier.

After a lot of back and forth and a number of calls from my mother, the builder decided he ought to come and see the distraught American woman. He entered our house, spotted the pots and the leaks and finally understood, "Ah, oka-san," he said, using the polite term the Japanese reserve for addressing the lady of the house. "It's raining IN the house."

Score one for international communication, but as I recall, things didn't improve much afterward. The house remained cold, dank, and dreary. But that was just the start of the troubles that plagued our house and contributed to my fearful state. There were lots of lizards—geckos. Some kids love lizards—but they are usually pets in a glass tank, not running around wild in the house like ours were. On Okinawa, a gecko creeping up the bedroom wall was considered a good thing—because they ate the bugs. And there were a lot of bugs. Really big ones. The worst were the cockroaches. Not the everyday thumbnail-sized cockroach that you might find in your kitchen. The huge ones, big enough to fly. The island—and our house—was infested with them. They were everywhere: in the furniture, in the shower, in the corners, on the ceiling. You never knew when you opened a drawer or a closet what would come flying or skittering out. I developed a lifelong terror of bugs. That first year there was also a shrew—a nasty sharp-toothed creature—hanging out one night in the bedroom Chris and I shared. My father donned his combat boots and chased after it with one of my brother's plastic toy golf clubs, which he wielded like a *Game of Thrones* broadsword.

But the most terrifying of the local wildlife was the venomous *habu*, a viper native only to Okinawa that seeks its prey in darkness. All the military families were warned about the *habu* as part of the orientation to Okinawa. Parents were instructed to have their kids play in the street (even with traffic!). It was safer dodging cars, they said, than going in the fields, because that's where the *habu*s often live. We were also told never to go out at night without a flashlight. The snakes were nocturnal, and would freeze in the beam of light. There were stories around the army base, repeated like ghost tales, of families' encounters with the *habu*. There was the family who found one living in their air conditioner. Another who found one on their back stoop. One night, when my mother opened the door, her flashlight revealed a fat five-foot *habu*, stippled with brown, yellow, and olive-green blotches. It fled the light and slithered into a hole in the stone wall around our house. Within an hour, there were police outside our house shining spotlights on the wall out front, searching for the deadly snake. They never found it. We spent the rest of the year warily scurrying past the spot where it had disappeared, eyes peeled for any movement in the rocks.

My new friends on Okinawa warned me of something else: quicksand. There was one field in particular that all the kids ominously pointed out and said we should never walk into. I would pass it every day on my way to school...gingerly testing the ground in front of me, terrified that at any step, it would suck me in and swallow me whole, never to be seen again.

When you are anxious in the way that I was, fears begin to feed on themselves. The feeling is so unpleasant that you start to notice *everything*, wondering if it is going to make you want to jump, wondering if you should run. I was poised at all times, it seems, to flee the bugs, the snakes, or a patch of marshy soil that looked like it might melt into quicksand. Even little things that normally don't bother people can send an anxious person up a wall. My brother was exposed to the same terrors as I was, but to me at least, he seemed to glide through, unperturbed.

Even my own body could frighten me. I remember having the hiccups one night, and I panicked. "Make it stop," I begged my parents. I could not understand it; why was this happening? "Beth, it's just hiccups," my parents tried to reassure me. They all called me Beth when I was growing up. "It will go away soon."

But I felt ambushed, as if something inside my body was actually taking over. Vomiting was even worse. Nobody likes it, but for me it wasn't just unpleasant but profoundly terrifying. It made me feel that I had lost complete control of my body, that it had been hijacked, and this triggered deep anxiety and a phobia about throwing up that I carry to this day. They were things I didn't understand, and at that age, children are often afraid of things they can't understand. We all carry our childhood selves with us as we go through life, and the little girl that still lives inside me needs, at the very least, to feel that she is in control of herself. I have since learned, through lots of therapy, that when fear is your default state of mind, you try very hard to control everything. It is a futile battle that can leave you exhausted, and desperate for relief.

We settled into our new lives on Okinawa. After six months, a home on base opened up, and we happily bade farewell to our little concrete house. By then I was in kindergarten, and we got our first beloved dog and named her Heidi. We grew up without watching television, so my parents read to us. I remember my mother reciting a nursery rhyme to me. "There was a little girl, who had a little curl, right in the middle of her forehead. When she was good, she was very very good. And when she was bad, she was horrid."

I had curls. Was this little girl me? Was I good? Was I horrid? I spent a lot of time thinking about that rhyme. Was it even possible to be both good and horrid?

It was during that second year in Okinawa that I first learned about death. I came home from school one day, and Heidi was not at the screen door as she usually was, jumping and yelping in happiness to see me. As I walked in the living room, it was quiet, and the air in the house felt heavy.

"Where's Heidi?" I asked my mom. I looked around for my brother, but I couldn't see him.

"Oh, Beth, I am so sorry," my mother said, sitting me down. "Heidi is dead." I struggled to comprehend. My eyes filled with tears as my mother gently explained what happened.

Heidi had run out of the house that day, when no one was looking, and was hit by a car. It was my brother who found her. My mother had discovered her four-year-old son sitting on the curb, crying, cradling Heidi's lifeless body. Chris was inconsolable. I looked around me, taking in the stillness and the emptiness. It was the first time I realized how fragile life was. Someone could be there one moment, and gone forever the next.

The world remembers 1969 as the year Neil Armstrong set foot on the moon. It certainly was a memorable event in our house: my mother woke Chris and me in the middle of the night and sat us down in front of our television to watch history being made in grainy black-and-white images. I remember looking out the window before crawling back into bed, staring at the moon. *That astronaut is up there,* I thought, *floating around this very moment.*

That year, 1969, was far more momentous for me because that was the year my father was sent to Vietnam.

By that time, I was six, and I knew even then it was dangerous there, and that bad things were happening. Fathers, brothers, and uncles died in wars. The only constants in my life at that point were my parents and my brother. There were no aunts or uncles or cousins living with us on Okinawa, no visits to our grandparents on holidays or just for Sunday dinner. We were nomads, our companions fleeting—other military families, who came and went as the army saw fit. We were in a country of people who spoke a different language and had a different culture.

The day in January when my father left for Saigon, we all went with him to the airport to say goodbye. My father held me close, and told me to be brave. My mother was now pregnant with my little sister, and I can only imagine how terribly frightening it must have been for her to see him get on that plane and leave her alone with two small children and a baby on the way. My father was so distraught, he was physically sick once he boarded the flight.

My mom took Chris and me to the officers' club on base to have dinner after my dad left. We sat there at the table, eating our fried rice while she sobbed, telling us it will be okay. I think she was trying to convince herself.

But I was definitely not okay. I responded to his departure with daily, full-blown panic attacks, a tsunami of anxiety, so intense that I felt I was about to die. There was absolutely nothing I could do to control it. The panic would envelop me, drown me. I was defenseless in the face of it. My heart would race; the blood pounded in my ears; my stomach churned.

Clearly something was not right inside me. My brother didn't have panic attacks. None of the other kids in the neighborhood appeared to have them...just me. My mother was forced to go to work that year—it was the only way we could stay on Okinawa, closer to my dad, who might be allowed to leave the war for a few days when my sister was born. Every single day, when my mother went to work, leaving my brother and me with our Japanese housekeeper, I panicked. If my father could disappear from my life, just like that, how did I know my mother would return?

Each morning, I would completely lose it: chasing after her, clinging to her legs, grasping at her skirt, sobbing, pleading, begging her not to go. I would dig in my heels, trying to stop her, forcing her to drag me along, my bare feet skidding across the stone walk to the car in the driveway. Every day it was the same. She'd barely manage to peel my fingers off her legs and get in the car and drive off, leaving me sobbing in the front yard.

Many years later, when I was in rehab, one of the counselors asked me, "What did your mother do to comfort you?"

"I can't remember," I said, "but I'm sure she did. Of course she did."

But when my mother came to visit me in rehab, I asked her about it. "How did you comfort me, Mom, when I had those panic attacks the year Dad was in Vietnam?"

"I didn't," she told me. "I felt so helpless. I didn't know how to help you."

My mother was just 28 that year, pregnant, with a husband at war. There was nowhere for her to turn for help. The army psychologists had their hands full with tens of thousands of Vietnam vets. The army wasn't even treating them for PTSD at the time. No one was thinking about the traumatized children.

Four months after my dad left, my mother gave birth to Aimie. It was nighttime. My brother was already asleep when my mom asked a neighbor to watch us while she went to the hospital. From the top bunk of the bunk bed I shared with Chris, I stared through the window, watching her walk toward the car, leaning over slightly, one hand on her stomach, the other clutching a small bag. As she opened the car door, it hit me: a wave of panic. I jumped out of bed, a high-pitched cry filled my ears, and I realized it was me. I ran toward the front door to try to stop her. It didn't matter that she needed to go to the hospital, that the baby was coming. I needed her, and I could not control myself. The neighbor stopped me before I could make it outside.

"Hey, hey, where are you going?" She stopped and looked closely at me. "What's the matter with you? Go to bed now. Stop making a scene."

It was at that moment that I realized that anxiety and panic were things I had to hide. Something in the way that neighbor looked at me made me feel ashamed of my galloping fear, my inability to hide or control it. On the night my sister Aimie was born, I learned a terrible and ultimately destructive lesson. No matter how huge the anxiety, no matter how powerful the panic, I must never, ever show it. No one can ever know. It was something weak and shameful, and it had to be hidden at all costs.

I still panicked in the mornings when my mom left, but I tried never to let anyone else see it. And I never, ever talked about my panic to anyone. I never confided in my brother. I did not tell my friends. I did not tell my first grade teacher, in whose class I arrived every day that last part of the school year, weary from my panic attack that morning. That teacher told my parents I was a delightful child, that I was bright and worked hard, and that I was one of her favorite students. By the summer of 1969, six months after my father went to war, I was different. My teachers in second grade and for many years after described me as quiet, withdrawn, with "a chip on her shoulder." Something within me was lost in Okinawa, never to be reclaimed.

—⚇—

Big Girls Don't Cry

When my dad came home from Vietnam, we returned to the United States for a few months, and then were sent right back overseas again to Germany.

Over the course of my childhood, I lived in fourteen different homes on nine different army bases and attended eight different schools—almost all of them overseas. Each year, everything changed. If we didn't move, most of our friends and neighbors did. The only constant was the five of us: my mother, my father, my brother, my sister, and me...and the U.S. Army.

We went where duty called, so the armed forces provided our family with its few islands of stability. No matter where in the world it is, every base is a little bit of the United States. There's a uniformity to military housing. All those cookie-cutter homes in a neat line. The same government-issue furniture. We all added some personal touches to our apartments. You could tell where a family had been stationed by the knickknacks they collected and unpacked after every move. Families with time in Germany had Hummels and cuckoo clocks. Those who had lived in

Asia hung beads in doorways and displayed bamboo trays on black lacquer chests. Wherever you went, though, one thing was always the same: the look and smell of the base commissary, where you bought eggs and ground beef and milk in half-gallon containers. Once you entered a PX, you could be anywhere—in Fort Leavenworth, Kansas; Frankfurt, Germany; or Livorno, Italy.

There were rituals to daily life in the armed forces. Reveille every morning, "Taps" at the close of day. The silent performance each afternoon as three soldiers gathered around the flagpole, two standing at attention while a third lowered the flag. Then their solemn, almost Zen movements as they assist in the folding of the Stars and Stripes, never letting it touch the ground. All of these aspects of growing up army instilled a lifelong feeling of patriotism at my core: a steady beacon in a landscape where the only constant was change.

My parents were determined not to be base bound. They wanted, even on my father's limited salary, to show us the world. We took many family trips together during our years stationed in Europe.

The five of us would pile into our tan two-door Maverick along with our new Dachshund, Gretel.

We were usually towing a camper behind the car, to save money on hotels. We would drive for days, with Aimie, Chris, and me crammed in the backseat—nudging, bickering, shoving, singing, and generally keeping up a nonstop level of background noise. We camped our way through the south of France and the beaches in Italy. We saw the tulips bloom in Holland and the art treasures of Florence. We learned to ski in Austria (we left the camper at home for that trip) and learned to slalom in Switzerland. It was an amazing gift our parents gave us. In those early years in Europe, I don't remember feeling anxious or worried, or having to fight panic. I think it was because we were all together. I felt safe.

That was not the case, however, when my parents took trips by themselves. That was hellish for me. They would leave us with friends for a week while they went to Paris or London. I would sit in the living room window, watching them drive away, the panic mounting in my throat. It took everything I had in me not to scream or cry and chase them down the street. I would endure the week they were gone, numbly going through the motions, always teetering right on the edge of completely losing it. My anxiety filled my body. I could not eat. The friends minding us would ask, "Are you okay? Aren't you hungry?" There was nothing anyone could say or do to make it better, and I felt I couldn't tell anyone how fragile and terrified I really felt. Naming that fear would give it even more power. I had learned in Okinawa to keep it hidden. I didn't say a word. I simply hung on and somehow endured until my parents came home. I remember my mom and dad used to sing a song to me when I was little, when I would get tearful. "Big girls, they don't cry, they don't cry…" It was the same lyric, over and over. They would sing and laugh and clap their hands. They were trying to distract me from whatever was making me upset, but it only made me frustrated. I thought they were mocking me and my tears. By the time I was eight, I embraced that refrain as a way of life. Don't cry. Don't show anyone you hurt.

I learned to run from my anxiety by losing myself in the imaginary world of books. I was a voracious reader. At school I would sit in the back of the classroom with one of my own books tucked inside whatever textbook we were supposed to be studying. I would read under the covers at night with a flashlight when we were supposed to be sleeping. I shed my worried, panicky self and took on the lives and the characters that captivated me. I imagined myself in all the girls' classics as if they were my own life. Who was I in *Little Women*? My namesake, Beth? Or Jo? Or Amy? I fell in love completely with *Anne of Green Gables*. Anne was the plucky orphan who not only survives but thrives despite tough challenges. I devoured the trilogy about her, wishing I too had red hair. When I got bored with the Nancy Drew series, my mother introduced me to Agatha Christie—the first book I read was *And Then There Were None*, though at that time it was still titled the politically incorrect *Ten Little Indians*. By the time I was nearly ten I was deeply immersed in reading about Henry VIII and his six wives. The glamour, the peril, the betrayal, the beheadings! I would dream that I was a reincarnation of the doomed Anne Boleyn, done in by her ambition and a ruthless Tudor court. At other times I would fantasize about traveling back in time and whispering in Anne's ear, "Your daughter Elizabeth will be one of England's greatest monarchs."

My parents took heart from my interest in books and my fascination with English history. For years, every birthday or Christmas meant a new doll from the court of Henry VIII—the massive king, all six of his wives, even the two princesses, Elizabeth and Mary. For a school project, I built the Tower of London out of paper towel tubes and cardboard, carefully painting it to look like a stone fortress. I was thrilled when on my tenth birthday my mom and dad surprised me with a fake British newspaper—the type you can buy at a shop selling tourist trinkets. The headline said HAPPY BIRTHDAY, BETH. We were going to London, just us! It was my first trip alone with them, and I felt special as we tramped to the big tourist sights: Westminster Abbey, Buckingham Palace, and, of course, the forbidding Tower, where Henry VIII would send wife number 2 (Anne Boleyn) and wife number 5 (Catherine Howard) to their execution. I hung on every word of our guide, who told us that on some nights, people swear they can hear Catherine Howard's screams as she was dragged to her appointment with the royal headsman. That trip meant so much to me. It brought my imaginary world alive, and that world had been my lifeline since we arrived in Germany.

*   *   *

The years since our move from Okinawa had been difficult. We moved to Stuttgart, in the middle of my third grade year, and friendships and cliques forged fast on army bases were solidified by the time I arrived. I was the outsider, nervous and lonely. I was very small for my age, and because we were seated alphabetically, I always sat in the very back. That year, I might as well have had a sign saying BULLY ME pinned to my back. I quickly became the prime target of the class queen bee, Andrea Powers.

Every day Andrea would threaten me, announcing to her gaggle of girls, "I'm gonna beat her up when the bus drops us off." So the second I stepped off the bus I'd run for dear life. Thank God I was fast. Fear can do that.

This went on for months. One day, my brother, who knew what was happening, came to the bus stop to meet me. I remember seeing him on his bike, waiting for me, his brown eyes searching for mine in one of the school bus windows. My heart sank. Instead of feeling comforted by his presence, I was ashamed. He could not protect me; he could only watch me running for my life, backpack flapping furiously behind me, just out of reach of Andrea's grasp. It never occurred to me to ask the bus driver for help or tell one of the teachers. I was utterly resigned to my place in the pecking order.

The bullying followed me, like a bad feeling you can't shake, even to the classroom. All my classmates were into playing jacks that year in third grade. I begged my parents to buy me a set. I brought them to school, brand new, still in their little felt bag. During the first free period, I proudly took them out and began to play. *Now I'll be just like the other girls. They'll see that and begin to like me.*

Instead, as I bounced my ball and scooped my jacks, Andrea walked over, raised her foot, paused for a second, and then slammed her foot down, crushing every one of my sparkly new jacks. I stared at the broken pieces. I didn't even look up. I knew that none of the other kids would defend me. I didn't utter a word of protest. I just sat there, heartbroken and embarrassed.

My mother had been bullied herself in school, and it broke her heart to see me go through it. She began writing me notes every day, hidden in my lunch box. They would be just a few words of encouragement and love, always signed with a smiley face. The lunch box notes helped a little. It was only after I became a mother myself that I realized how hard that must have been for her. She now wishes she had marched over to Andrea Powers's house—it was just a few blocks away on base—and read her mother the riot act.

Andrea was the first of many bullies I had to contend with over the course of my childhood, in a series of schools scattered from Germany to Kansas. They were always cut from the same cloth: queen bee girls, "it girls" with long limbs and curtains of blond hair who were always whispering mean-girl gossip behind my back—and sometimes in front of me.

I became convinced that if I only just looked different, more like everyone else, I would fit in. I was always too small, and I had thick, unruly hair. I hated it.

All I wanted was long, straight hair, not this chaos of short black curls that would not lay flat, no matter how hard I tried to make it so. In seventh grade I came up with the bright idea to Scotch tape my bangs to my forehead as they dried in the morning, to keep them straight. It worked, sort of. But then one morning I forgot to take the tape off before I walked to the bus stop. I stood for ten minutes smiling nervously as kids stared quizzically, a few smirking, before somebody said, "Hey, you might want to take the Scotch tape off your forehead."

Great. Ditch the Scotch tape. My lack of self-esteem was compounded by the fact that I was a late bloomer. So, when all the other girls were developing curvy hips and wearing bras, I was still skinny and flat chested. One day, in early adolescence—when we lived in Kansas—I was feeling reasonably good about myself and even kind of proud of my new school clothes. The pride evaporated when the queen bee of the class sat down beside me and brought me down to earth. "Beth, you shouldn't lean forward with your blouse open when you sit like that," she said in a phony-friendly way.

"Why?"

"Because everyone can see that you stuffed your bra with green Kleenex."

With each move, to each new school on each new army base, I prayed that I could conquer my worries and insecurity, and reinvent myself. *This time I'll find the magic formula. This time I'll figure out the rulebook that everyone else obviously lives by but no one ever showed me. And then, if I act a certain way, or dress a certain way, I'll fit in.*

My anxiety, as always, was lurking in the corner of my eye. As I grew older, and bigger, it seemed to grow along with me...and began slipping out, no matter how hard I tried to suppress it. I began to feel anxious when my family took day trips away from home, although I didn't recognize at the time that was what I was feeling. In contrast to the sense of security of being with my family that I felt when we piled into the car and went on camping trips in Europe, when I was in early adolescence and we lived at Fort Leavenworth, weekend outings in Kansas City took a different turn. We would pile into our white station wagon, and drive to the city for a little window-shopping and a pizza—nothing that out of the ordinary. You'd think I'd look forward to a change of scene from Fort Leavenworth, but by this time my anxiety had progressed to the point that leaving the familiarity of the base rattled me. I would get nauseous all the way to Crown Center, triggering my vomit phobia, further rousing my anxiety. I'd sit in the backseat clutching a paper bag, my face pressed against the window, praying the queasiness would pass. Hours later, as soon as the car pointed back toward the army base, the nausea would suddenly, miraculously, be gone, leaving me wrung out but relieved to be heading home. It was only decades later that I learned that feeling of needing to vomit is a classic manifestation of anxiety in many people.

The dogged daily battle with anxiety had one unexpected and positive result. It made me tougher. I didn't like fighting with my fears every day as if my very life depended on it, but doing so gave me a resolve, an inner reserve that would serve me well.

My adventure in cheerleading was a good example. It started in Germany as I went out for the squad when my brother was playing Pee Wee football: a nostalgic slice of Americana on the playing fields of an army base in the middle of Europe.

At the cheerleading tryouts I was a complete washout: timid and afraid, incapable of lifting my gaze from the ground five feet in front of me, a far cry from the high-spirited and perky attitude that puts the *cheer* in *cheerleader*. Not surprisingly, I didn't make the cut. My mother tried to comfort me.

"It's okay, Beth," my mom said. "Just try harder next year."

I spent the next twelve months practicing cheers, doing the splits, and making eye contact with the imaginary judges in front of me.

The next year, I was picked for the squad, and for every other cheerleading group all the way through high school. My skill at gymnastics worked in my favor. I loved launching handsprings across the football field or, later, the basketball court, or balancing on top of a human pyramid in front of the crowd. It was the first time in my life that instead of shutting down with my anxiety, I turned and faced it head-on, and won.

Cheerleading gave me the social entrée that had eluded me ever since first grade. All of sudden I was no longer the shy outsider who got picked on. I was part of a group. I had the novel experience of feeling accepted, even kind of cool. For the first time, I fit in, joining in normal teenage activities as we moved back to the States, to Fort Leavenworth, Kansas: hanging out at the mall, going to the movies, checking out the boys in the parking lot at McDonald's, and, to my surprise and delight, being checked out by the boys in return.

Those last years in high school, we moved back to Germany, to a small base in Heidelberg. They were relatively happy years. Like many kids, I tried drinking, but only in tiny sips. I was frightened of feeling out of control. The local gasthauses did not check our IDs and were happy to serve teenagers beer and wine and apple schnapps. My parents never worried about me drinking too much, like some of the other kids who got caught. They knew how terrified I was of vomiting. "We never have to worry about you getting drunk like some of your friends," they would laugh. "You are too afraid you might throw up!"

I was smart enough to be placed in all the AP English

classes, but I coasted academically, until the end of junior year, when a school-wide scandal shook me awake. That year, the varsity basketball team was in a tournament, and the cheerleaders decided to have a slumber party to paint signs and make streamers.

We all said there would be parents at the house where we stayed that night. We lied. We stayed up late, blasting Sister Sledge and Dire Straits on the stereo, baking cupcakes for the football team, and taking turns frying our faces under a sun lamp. We ended up oversleeping, and by the time we arrived at the school, with our pom-poms and cupcakes, our faces blistered and swollen, the team bus had already gone. The whole varsity cheerleading squad missed the tournament and got into big trouble. Our night of baking—both our faces and the cakes—suddenly morphed into a night of unsupervised partying in the whispered accounts in the school halls. We were threatened with suspension. And for whatever reason, the teacher who was in charge of us blamed everything on me. To this day I am not sure why, but it was clear then and in the following year, that she had it in for me.

It was wrong, and I knew it. I was shocked that an adult would target me this way. I was accustomed to classroom bullies, but they were always other kids, not members of the faculty.

That teacher pulled my mother aside at that time.

"Beth's not college material," she said. "You should make her stay home after graduating next year. Then you can see if any school will accept her." My mother was furious. She knew that woman was wrong, and she told her so before abruptly walking out.

It was then, at the end of my junior year, when I made up my mind. It was time to focus and get to work. I quit the cheerleading squad. I buckled down in my studies. I was nominated to be editor of the high school newspaper. That same teacher actually tried to block me, but the other faculty overruled her. (What an awful woman she was!) I worked hard my senior year and discovered I loved writing and reporting. I wrote most of the articles in our newspaper myself, and then cut and pasted the layout each week on my dining room table before taking it to the printer.

It was that year, my last at home in high school, when I realized what I wanted to become in life: a journalist.

I was accepted to college, proving that teacher wrong, and it was one of the best schools of journalism in the country: the University of Missouri. My parents packed me on a plane in Germany and sent me, all by myself, to a school I had never seen (no college tours for us) and where I didn't know a soul. I was panicked when I left, and unbearably homesick when I arrived. I would not see my family again until Christmas. I could not afford to call Germany. I could only spend the next four and a half months writing tearful letters home.

As I began that first, difficult semester, two sides of my character were set: driven by anxiety, panicked that it would show my fundamental weakness, and—on the other hand—an ability to buckle down, set goals, and achieve them. All through college and then on up the rungs of the career ladder in broadcast journalism—progressing from smaller to ever larger markets—I was able to keep my anxiety hidden, sometimes just barely. No one knew it was there, except me. And for many years no one knew I was drinking to keep it at bay, until the alcohol turned on me.

PART II

The Big Stage

It was a brilliant autumn morning, the kind that inspires poets and painters. The air was crisp and the sky was cobalt blue, and downtown in lower Manhattan, the Twin Towers were burning. I stared in horror at the TV screen, unable to properly process what I was seeing. I listened as Diane Sawyer and Charlie Gibson described how two planes loaded with passengers had crashed—one into each tower—and that the United States was under attack. I could barely move. I could not believe what I was seeing. *Are those people jumping from those buildings?* The enormity of the tragedy was incomprehensible. The events of the day were still unfolding, but the suicide bombers on those four hijacked planes would carry out the most devastating attack on our nation's soil since Pearl Harbor. Like millions of people, I will never forget exactly where I was standing, and how the room felt frozen as I watched those towers, engulfed in flames, knowing people were dying. I will also never forget that on that searing morning, I was hungover. Really hungover. Dry mouth, swollen eyes, shaky hands hungover.

The night before, my future husband Marc and I went

to the premiere of a movie, written and directed by a friend of his. The dinner party afterward was at the 21 Club, a vintage New York restaurant favored by the city's power players. The ceilings are low and the tables are always packed and close together. It was a lovely dinner with the director and his cast, with plenty of wine poured by attentive waiters. When I got home, I kept the evening going, talking to my parents, who were visiting and preparing to leave early the next day. We stayed up several hours more, drinking more wine. By the time I went to bed at two a.m. on September 11, I had been drinking slowly but steadily for six hours. And now, in the bright morning light at nine thirty, I was paying the price. I grabbed a bottle of water to rehydrate and went back to the television. Information started coming in. The doomed airplanes were all United or American Airlines passenger jets, headed to the west coast from the east coast. I panicked and dropped my water. My parents were on an American flight that morning from JFK to San Francisco. I dumped the contents of my purse on the floor, frantically searching for the paper with their flight number on it, then sat back on my heels holding it in my hand waiting for Diane and Charlie to tell the flight numbers of the hijacked planes. It felt like forever, but finally I learned my parents' plane was not one of those hijacked. But I had no idea where they were, if they had boarded, if they had taken off before all flights in our nation were grounded that day. They did not have a cell phone. I could only wait for them to call. But now, I needed to get to work. I threw on some clothes and raced down to the ABC studios. Peter Jennings had taken over the live coverage by then. It was he who stopped everyone from talking when the Twin Towers began to crumble and fall. There was a horrified hush throughout our teeming newsroom, in the control room and on the set, as we watched thousands of people lose their lives that very moment. The Pentagon, that field in Pennsylvania... it was all so brutally unreal.

By the time I arrived at ABC, other correspondents were already on the scene of the devastation downtown. I was asked to remain at the studio in case Peter Jennings needed to take a break. I had anchored other breaking news events in the past already—several hours without break on the day John F. Kennedy Jr.'s plane crashed at sea, and again when the FBI raided a Florida home to return Elian Gonzales to Cuba and ended an international stalemate. It could be true that they needed me there that day to spell Peter. But I feared the assignment editors could see how horrible I felt. I spent a few hours drinking Gatorade, logging images, taking notes, and praying no one would notice me. In late afternoon, I was told I would anchor ABC's round-the-clock coverage overnight—relieving Peter at eleven p.m. Eastern time, anchoring until *Good Morning America* came on the air the next morning. I went home, ostensibly to get some rest before the overnight shift, but also to finally sleep off that now-distant celebration of the night before.

The next few days felt surreal. We all worked nonstop.

I went down to the Pile, as they called it, the wreckage of the towers that spanned blocks, still smoking, the ashes and bits of paper still floating through the air. Rescuers and their dogs crouched deep in the massive debris, straining to hear any sound of life underneath. We all prayed for a miracle, that someone beneath would make a noise and the rescuers could pull a person free. That didn't happen nearly enough. The stories we told in those days were simply heartbreaking. I held it together until the third day, September 14. Late in the afternoon, desperate to clear my head, I grabbed my sneakers from my desk drawer and went out for a run in Central Park, a block away from the office. I was jogging around the Reservoir, breathing in its serene beauty. It was clear, crisp, and oddly quiet. The skies over the nation were still closed to international flights, our borders still sealed. I had never experienced a day in Manhattan without the drone of jumbo jets lumbering nonstop overhead. Suddenly, the silence was pierced by the deafening roar of fighter jets. I stopped jogging and looked up at a pair of F-15s streaking across the sky, flying straight up the center of Manhattan.

They were heading south directly overhead, and for some reason that's when it really hit me: we had been attacked. Our skies are being patrolled. We are at war. I stopped, leaned over with my hands on my knees, and cried.

It would be years before I would look back at the

attacks on 9/11 and see that in the unprecedented, tragic events of that terrible day, there was a tiny hidden message for me, one that said *it is not normal to be that hungover in the morning*. Normal people don't need to drink several glasses of wine to feel comfortable at a dinner party or to talk to their own parents. What are you drinking to escape: the anxiety? Or yourself?

But my slide into problem drinking was very slow and very gradual. It didn't make a scene or scream out for attention. After 9/11, it receded into the background for a few years, before making a spectacular return to center stage.

My professional life to that point had been a successful climb through the ranks of broadcast journalism. I had attended one of the best journalism schools in the country and went on to work in local news, moving quickly from smaller markets to bigger ones: first Reno, then Phoenix, on to Chicago, before arriving in New York and the national stage. I worked for three years as a correspondent for *Dateline*, and filled in as co-host of the *Today* show on NBC before jumping to ABC in 1996. My career had thus far been one of unbroken ascent. To all outward appearances, I was an effective and dedicated journalist carving out a significant place for myself: calm, composed, with unwavering focus. Inside, however, I was still as anxious and insecure as ever—certain someone would surely see that I was in over my head and that my confidence and professionalism was a façade.

I was very happy at NBC and might have stayed there for my entire career had Roone Arledge, one of the most powerful, innovative, and persuasive network executives in the history of television, not come knocking at my door. Roone was the man who created the Olympics as a non-stop prime-time extravaganza (and ratings behemoth). He oversaw the creation of *Monday Night Football*, *20/20*, and *Nightline*. He was a programming genius.

Would I be interested, he asked, in coming over to ABC to possibly take over for Joan Lunden as co-host of *Good Morning America*?

Who wouldn't say yes? I didn't ask any of the important questions, like *Does Joan know you want to replace her? How will she, and the rest of the team, feel about my arrival?* I blithely signed up, thrilled with the potential opportunity to do more of the live morning television I had grown to love filling in for Katie Couric on *Today*.

GMA had slipped in the ratings to number 2, and with tens of millions of dollars in advertising at stake, network executives were intent on turning things around.

When I arrived in the spring of 1996, there was already a shake-up under way. *GMA* had always been in the entertainment division of the company, but shortly before I came over from NBC, Roone took over *GMA* and moved it to the news division. Personnel changed; management was let go; people lived in fear for their jobs. I was the first hire from the news division, replacing a veteran newsman, Morton Dean, who was highly respected and well loved. I had no idea what I was walking into, and I wasn't experienced enough or mature enough to pay attention. Some staff at the show resented my arrival, and I only made matters worse because I was oblivious to what was going on and was easily offended at the cool greeting I received. It was all exacerbated by the breathless reports in the newspapers that I was there to replace Joan. She was still very popular with many viewers and staff, and she was understandably upset at the speculation that she was on her way out.

I learned I was not welcome on my first morning there, when I was ushered to a tiny room to do my research and get into hair and makeup. The rest of the cast were all in the big, bright room down the hall, filled with laughter and preshow bonding.

There were some other unpleasant events—one morning someone taped a paper with the word *bitch* written on it to my chair, and unflattering stories about me started leaking to the gossip pages.

Joan had been a big star for many years. I, on the other hand, was framed as an ambitious, younger upstart. It was a classic *All about Eve* scenario. All this media attention was new to me and bewildering. At NBC I was a peon; nobody had ever once written a story about me in my career. My job was to report the news, not make it.

But the jump to ABC had set off a frenzy of rumors and backbiting fueled by anonymous sources.

I was rattled and defensive. It felt like I was back in third grade, only I wasn't sure who the bully was this time. I began having panic attacks again, a handful of times, on the air. I would have a hard time catching my breath and would feel nauseous, terrified I would vomit. "I have a touch of the flu," I would gasp to my producer, Dan Woo. He was a wonderful man, and he was singularly kind to me every day.

"Just tell me how I can help you," he would say. "We'll get you through this."

I never told him it was anxiety, not the flu, even though he knew what was going on each morning and may have understood why I was anxious. I could not trust my secret with anyone. It would make me too vulnerable. Someone might say, "Oh! Well, people who have panic attacks don't belong on live TV! Get a different job."

It wasn't the first time my anxiety took hold of me and shook me like a rag doll. I had a terrible attack a few years earlier, in Chicago, while anchoring the ten p.m. newscast on a Saturday night at WBBM. I was alongside a veteran anchor, Mike Parker. As the show started, my heart began to pound. I am not sure what set my panic off that night. Possibly I had too much food in my stomach. I like to eat very little before going on camera, just enough so I don't get shaky from hunger. Too much food, and I feel full and get anxious. It was a little like Goldilocks: not too little, not too much. I might have been tired, not feeling quite right.

During the first block of the newscast (approximately seven minutes), I began to feel like I couldn't get enough air. I couldn't speak, and I felt queasy. My hands started to tremble. At some point, I was sure I was going to vomit. I clenched my jaws together and stopped reading the script, fighting the urge to throw up. Thank God we were reading live to prerecorded video, so the audience couldn't see my distress. Mike, however, saw me freeze and shut down: after a few seconds of dead air—no one talking when I was supposed to—he jumped in and read my part. When we went to commercial the producer asked, "Are you okay?" I could hear the concern in her voice. Mike was not as understanding. I had just left him holding the bag on live television. He turned and looked at me with disbelief. "What the *fuck* is wrong with you?" he said.

Minus the expletive, they were the exact words that our neighbor in Okinawa had said to me when I panicked as my mom left to give birth to my sister. Twenty years later, the message was still the same. *You are wrong to feel this. It is embarrassing. Hide this at all costs.*

At ABC, panic didn't just strike me while on live television. It happened at other times, too, once in particular during my first year there. Every fall, the network hosted a luncheon at Tavern on the Green for its important major advertisers. Every prominent journalist at the network was seated at a table with several of these advertising VIPs and instructed to be charming. Halfway through the meal, *World News Tonight* anchor Peter Jennings would take to the stage and talk about current affairs and politics, and then ask each of the anchors and correspondents a question about news events or stories they had recently done. All the big names were there: Barbara Walters, Diane Sawyer, Sam Donaldson, Ted Koppel, Connie Chung. Each one, when called on by Peter, stood up, took the microphone from their table, and, with all the confidence in the world, winged these beautifully crafted, often funny, and always insightful answers.

My turn came at the end, and by then I was a basket case—all my insecurity was raging. *I am not as smart as Barbara and Diane. I am not as charming as Connie. What am I doing here?* I can't remember what Peter asked me, but as I reached for the microphone I was shaking so badly I actually could not stand. I stayed seated, even as others motioned to me to get up. I gripped the mic with both hands. Peter's question had something to do with the military and their families, so I told the story of my dad going to Vietnam, about the effect it had on my mother and Chris and me. I explained how conflicted my dad felt about the war, how he came to believe we had no business being in Vietnam (in later years my mother told me that he had almost resigned from the army at this point). I rambled on. I don't know what I said, but it made some kind of impression on Roone Arledge. A few days later, he pulled me aside. "What you said at that lunch was impressive. Well done."

Many years later Peter Jennings surprised me when he referred to my father's time in the army. I looked at him quizzically. "How did you know my dad was in the army?"

"I remember you speaking about it when you first came here," he said. I was amazed and impressed that he remembered my rambling, panicky remarks that day. Praise of any kind from Peter was to be treasured. He was smart, and tough, and dedicated. He did not suffer fools gladly. If he said something was good, you could take it to the bank. Years later I filled in for him, anchoring *World News Tonight* for a week while he was on vacation. When he returned he sent me an email: "Nice job last week." That was it. But coming from Peter, that was a lot. I was over the moon.

That first year and a half at ABC, while I was at *GMA*, drinking was never a problem. You simply couldn't get up at four thirty a.m. and do your job if you drank too much. I limited myself to one glass a night. A daily glass or two of wine had become a habit after work since my earliest days in the business. The only difference was, in the beginning, when I was usually broke, I poured my nightly glass of discount wine out of a box. By the time I got to *GMA* I could afford to uncork a chilled bottle of buttery California chardonnay, or a crisp French Chablis. Wine helped me quiet the insecurity that had been with me since I was a girl. It never occurred to me to seek professional help. I had never in my life discussed my anxiety with anyone, not a soul. I didn't talk to my mom about it, even though I had chased her down the driveway in full-blown panic. I still believed it was shameful, a weakness. Talking about it would somehow make the fear and insecurity more tangible, more real. It never occurred to me that other people in the world might feel the same way. The idea of seeing a therapist about it was so foreign to me you might as well have suggested I go to the moon to learn how to manage my anxiety. I didn't grow up in the kind of home where we talked a lot about our feelings, or our fears, and it is hard to describe a panic attack to someone who has never suffered one. All I can say even today is that when it hits, you feel you cannot breathe, your heart feels like it will explode it is pounding so hard and so fast. I often fear I will vomit, that my body will sprint far away from my control—that terror will hijack every single part of me and make me flail or scream or do something even more embarassing. Once, when I was eleven, my family was camping in France. Chris, Aimie, and I were at a playground with all the other children at the campsite, pantomiming to communicate with the kids from other countries. Suddenly, my little sister tumbled from the swing set, hitting the gravel path hard, face-first. She stood up, screaming in shock and fright, tears streaming down her cheeks, blood gushing down her chin. She came running straight toward me, her arms out. And in that moment, I panicked. I turned and ran for our mother. My anxiety overrode my capacity to think, or to help her. My love for my sister was not calling the shots for my brain and my body. My panic was, and it told me to run away from her. That is what a panic attack does. Your body takes over. You reflexively flee whatever it is that is terrifying to you, even when it's just your hurt little sister who desperately needs you.

With my wine consumption curtailed on the early shift, my main way to keep the anxiety at bay was to work out— sometimes twice a day during that time. I'd run in the park, or hit the treadmill and Stairmaster, sweating and stewing about what I could do to make things go better at *GMA*. I was working hard, but the plain fact is that I was miserable at the art of office politics and developing allies. I was naïve, and too insecure to ask anyone for help. At the level of the game I was playing, this proved to be my Achilles heel.

By the summer of 1997, the *GMA* drama was in its final throes. Yes, Joan Lunden was going to be replaced, as long rumored. But not by me. The job instead went to Lisa McCree, a local anchor from Los Angeles with short blond hair and a big, sunny smile. It was a painful time. I was humiliated that after all the ballyhoo about me replacing Joan, I had been snubbed. I tried not to read all the news stories and the speculation about why I was passed over. I focused on the new job I was assigned at the network—as a correspondent for the news magazine shows *20/20* and *Primetime Live.* I pretended everything was fine, that my fragile confidence had not been shaken, and that every secret fear I nurtured had not just been confirmed.

Liberated from the four a.m. alarm clock, I began drinking more, partly to numb my disappointment and partly because I had begun dating a well-known movie actor who was interesting, exciting, and very much liked to drink. I dated this man on and off for two years, and he was very, very disciplined when he was shooting a movie. When he wasn't, we drank. Nights out with him usually started with a martini at his apartment. I had never had one before. Martinis seemed so elegant and soigné: the beads of condensation on the cocktail shaker; the muffled click of the ice cubes, like a pair of dice that you shake in your hand before you roll them; and the stemware with its triangular silhouette. We would go out and order a bottle of wine with dinner, and a brandy with dessert.

One weekend, we were in Vienna, where he was being honored. Afterward, we flew in his plane to Spain, to his vacation house. When we boarded, there was a big bowl of caviar, cooling in crushed ice, and a big bottle of vodka.

We ate and drank it all before the plane landed two hours later.

I had never drunk alcohol like this before, and I took to it. It was a welcome distraction from my disappointment at work. I didn't feel quite so insecure when I was with him, toasting the sunset in Majorca with our chilled goblets of Spanish wine. And I didn't even think I was drinking excessively. Everyone else around us, our friends, our dinner companions, all seemed to drink the same way.

But someplace, way deep down inside, I must have known I was going overboard. On my birthday that year, as I was heading out of the office to meet this man and some friends, my assistant called out after me. "Have fun! Don't drink too much!"

I nearly stopped in my tracks. Why would she say that? Does she think I drink too much? Do people know I am out drinking every night? Or was that just an innocent pleasantry? I couldn't tell. I still don't know. But she definitely hit a nerve. I didn't want to be known for that—for drinking too much. That would be horrible. I think that night I cut back, but just a tiny bit.

In my new position at *20/20*, I traveled a lot, all around the world. Frequent flying comes with the territory when you are a network correspondent, but I hated flying. Those airplane trips that seemed so exotic and exciting when I was a child were now stressful. I felt claustrophobic on planes, completely out of control—probably because I was. I had grown to hate being in confined spaces when I could not get out. When I first came to New York, I avoided the subways in rush hour, because squeezing into a crowded train that often stopped in the middle of the tunnel would send me into a full panic. I didn't like elevators, either— the rides up and down were something I endured when I could not take the stairs; during every trip in one, I was tense, poised to completely lose it if the doors were too slow to open.

But airplane rides were the worst: unavoidable, and hours long. On one flight, I did actually panic. My heart was pounding so fast I thought I would die of a heart attack, and I was sweating and shaking. I needed to get out—*now*. I got through it by asking for a glass of wine, but it left me shaken. What if, crazy with anxiety, I had tried to open the airplane door? I went to my doctor and, for the first time, told someone about my panic. He gave me an anti-anxiety prescription that I carried everywhere. I never took the pills, not then, at least. But just knowing I had them with me and could take one if I needed to was a comfort.

That, and the wine I was now ordering on every flight. It wasn't always anxiety driving me to ask for another glass; it was sometimes boredom. Flights were more fun when you had a little buzz. I thought nothing wrong in drinking while flying, plus everyone else in business class was ordering a Scotch on the rocks or a beer before takeoff.

It was insidious and slow, this habit I was developing to calm myself with wine—no longer just after work, but any time I felt anxious, or bored. It was only a matter of time before the occasions in my life that "would clearly be better with a chardonnay" stretched and expanded, and began to encompass other more mundane hours in my day.

—⟨⟩—

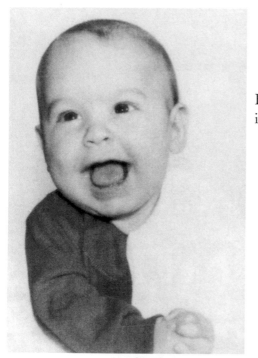

Born a "Jersey Girl"
in 1962.

A happy time
with my father
in Okinawa.

Christmas in Okinawa—with my brother, Chris—before Dad left for war.

Posing in front of a palm tree in 1969. With my father at war, I was panicking daily.

A drawing I gave my father as he left for Vietnam. He told me not to cry (big girls don't cry!). He kept that piece of paper in his pocket the whole year he was at war.

Anchoring ABC's *World News Tonight*. Before my first line, I would always take a deep breath, and grip the desk hard, to stay focused. *(ABC/Ida Mae Astute)*

Reporting from Israel. I was afraid of flying, especially the long flights, and felt tense throughout those trips. *(ABC/Donna Svennevik)*

With my parents on my wedding day. I was so happy, and had such high hopes.

Reporting from Baghdad, Iraq, in 2005 after I just found out I was pregnant with Sam. *(ABC News/Vinnie Malhotra)*

Co-anchoring with Bob Woodruff on the expanded version of ABC's *World News Tonight* in 2006. *(Credit: ABC/Jeff Neira)*

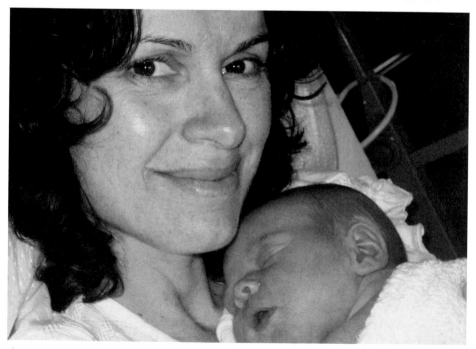

At the hospital with two-day-old Sam. He was big and beautiful and blond...he was absolutely perfect.

Pictured with President George W. Bush during my visit to the White House in 2006. I was a bundle of nerves when I arrived, but the interview went smoothly, and President Bush and I chatted for well beyond the allotted twenty minutes. It was extraordinary. *(Eric Draper)*

Guest-hosting *Good Morning America*. We were reacting to a message from Robin Roberts, who was on medical leave. Later I would pick George Stephanopolous to interview me for a tell-all sit-down interview. (L–R: Sam Champion, Josh Elliott, Me, George Stephanopolous) *(ABC/Fred Lee)*

Pictured with my *20/20* co-host, David Muir—who had been one of the most supportive people during my time at rehab. *(ABC/Donna Svennevik)*

Ready for Primetime

By early 1999 I had grown to truly relish my new job on *20/20*. I loved magazine work—we had ten minutes, instead of two or three, to tell a story. Sometimes we had the whole hour. I was also anchoring *World News Tonight Saturday* and contributing stories to *GMA*. The actor and I had amicably called it quits, and I spent most of that summer happily hanging out with my friends Dana, Michelle, and Lori. We did everything together—walking their dogs in the park, going out to dinner, seeing concerts, and, oh yes, drinking.

None of us was dating anyone at the time, and I, at least, liked being single and completely unattached. As the city emptied out, everyone escaping the oppressive Manhattan heat, the four of us had our pick of the tables at popular restaurants. Some nights we would sit outside on Dana's deck, the city lights twinkling around us, sipping our wine and eating our take-out sushi. I loved that summer. The friendships we forged in those steamy months would last for years.

Because I had to anchor the news on Saturdays, I sometimes passed up the Friday nights of fun. So it was that on July 16, 1999, I was sitting in my window seat, watching the sun set, sipping my wine, listening to Shawn Colvin singing "Sunny Came Home" on the stereo. There was something strange about the sky...I had never seen it look this way. There was a thick haze blanketing the horizon, smudging the sun. I couldn't see where the water on the Hudson River ended and the sky—a dense, dirty orange—began.

I sat and watched the odd scene for more than an hour, until it was dark, and I got my things ready for work the next day.

The next morning, early, the phone rang as I was on my way out the door to the gym. It was my producer at *World News Tonight*. "We need you in here now. JFK Jr.'s plane has disappeared. We are going to go live as soon as you can get here." I grabbed my work clothes and hopped in a cab. All the way there, I kept thinking another call would come in at any moment with my producer saying, "False alarm. They found it—everyone's fine."

But when I walked into the studio I could see everything was not fine. It was humming with activity, with urgency. John Kennedy; his wife, Carolyn; and her sister Lauren had taken off in a single-engine plane from Essex County Airport in New Jersey the night before, headed for a family wedding on Martha's Vineyard. They were flying in that thick, soupy haze I had been transfixed with last night. And now they were lost.

My producer thrust research into my hands as my

makeup artist tried to powder my face. "We don't have time for this. You have to go on now," she said.

I ran to the set and pinned my microphone to my jacket. In my ear, the director talked through my IFB, "We are going on in fifteen seconds. Are you ready?"

No. I wasn't ready. I was nervous. I tucked my hair behind my ear and scanned the research and the flight data in front of me. "Plane disappeared en route to Hyannisport...thick fog...no visibility...26 family members expected at the Vineyard...last radar shows plane descending at nearly 4,700 feet/minute...no deaths confirmed, but little hope for survivors." My God, I think, this is bad.

There were no scripts, no teleprompter. I would be ad-libbing live.

My heart was pounding. *Slow down, breathe,* I told myself. *Don't talk too fast. Focus. Concentrate.*

The stage manager has begun the countdown. "Seven, six, five..."

"Just give me bullet points," I tell the producers. "Slide it to me while I am on, highlight the important information."

"Three, two, one...and we're up."

As I anchored that day, I thought about the Kennedy family and how much tragedy they have endured. The search on the Atlantic that morning seemed surreal. Kennedy's cousin, Anthony Radziwill, had worked at ABC, and I had met John and Carolyn Bessette several times. I think we were all hoping there would be a call from another airport, where they had all safely landed, trying to escape that turgid haze the night before.

I anchored that day for several hours, without a commercial break. It took about 10 minutes for my anxiety to subside, for my heart rate to slow down, and for my hands to stop trembling. I had to wait until then to take a sip of the hot water with lemon that the crew had readied for me. I didn't dare pick up the cup before then, because my hands were still shaking and everyone in the control room, not to mention millions of viewers, would have seen it.

During those hours I interviewed emergency crews who were organizing the search, witnesses at the airport who saw the small plane leave, and historians who could not believe this latest turn in the Kennedy saga.

John Nance, our aviation expert, was on for much of the time as we analyzed the flight's last moments on radar. "Well, we can tell from the flight data that the plane was descending at a very rapid rate," he pointed out. My job was to think like the viewers and ask the questions they might ask. I posed the question that was on everyone's mind. "At that rate of descent, John, would it have been possible for Kennedy to pull up? Could he have avoided crashing into the ocean if he had seen it in time?" It was becoming clear that in last night's surreal haze, JFK had lost sight of the horizon, and was unknowingly on a trajectory taking the small plane on an angle down to the ocean, instead of flying parallel to it. We were all still desperately hoping this would end well.

After several hours, Peter Jennings arrived to take over. There was no handoff; I simply threw to a commercial, and when we came back on the air, Peter was at the desk.

"I'm Peter Jennings in New York, taking over for Elizabeth Vargas, who has been with you for the past several hours. We continue our coverage of John F. Kennedy's plane, which has disappeared overnight."

We all know how this story ends. U.S. Navy warships searched for days for survivors or wreckage. It was not until July 20 that the plane and the remains of its three passengers were found on the ocean floor. President Clinton told the nation, "The Kennedys had suffered much, and given more."

That was the first time I had ever anchored a live breaking news event for ABC. I learned that sad Saturday that I could conquer my anxiety in a clutch situation, and I earned back some of the confidence I had lost in my first difficult year at ABC.

I would go on to anchor many more breaking news events, live, with only my wits and the incredible staff and contributors of ABC news. Nine months later I anchored on another Saturday for hours without scripts or commercial breaks when U.S. federal agents raided a home in Miami and seized a terrified five-year-old boy named Elian Gonzalez. He had been found five months earlier clinging to an inner tube three miles off the coast of Fort Lauderdale. His mother and eleven others had drowned in their attempt to flee Cuba and join relatives in Florida.

An international stalemate had erupted. Elian's father and the Castro regime were demanding his return. Elian's aunt, uncle, and cousins in Miami were refusing to hand him over. In the early morning hours on April 22, 2000, the feds moved in. I remember being at the anchor desk that morning, and seeing for the first time the infamous photo of the burly agent in a bulletproof vest, machine gun drawn, and the terrified little boy in the crosshairs, backed up against a bedroom closet. Elian's eyes were wide with fear, his mouth opened as he screamed. I knew as soon as I saw that photo there would be a backlash—that the agents would be accused of being heavy-handed, of going too far. It was astonishing that this international tug-of-war over a little boy would end this way. Once again that day, I conquered my anxiety and anchored our coverage with authority and empathy. Our team won an Emmy for Outstanding Coverage of a Breaking News Event for our work. It was ironic that I would win my first network Emmy as anchor. All through my years at local affiliates, I was told that I was a lousy anchor. In a way, this turned out to be a blessing, because it forced me to develop my skills as a reporter. It was the years of reporting in local news—on plane crashes, hurricanes, household fires, robberies, political triumphs and downfalls—that brought me to the network level. Only then was I prepared to take on the high-wire act of anchoring breaking news. It's exhilarating, exciting, and furiously paced. It terrified me, yet I loved it. I was able in those moments to shove my anxiety to the side and focus like a laser beam on the major event that was happening and was bigger and so much more important than whatever nerves I might be battling.

I began to realize that it was in the most demanding circumstances as an anchor, when the wire was at its highest, I was somehow able to be my very best. That skill I learned early on, way back in Germany, to face what was frightening and lean into it, was now serving me well. It was a skill I would need again, when the personal stakes were so much higher.

—〰—

A Chance Encounter

One of my favorite New York events is the U.S. Open every September. It's gorgeous out at Arthur Ashe Stadium, in Queens. And the most elite tennis players in the world come to compete for a Grand Slam title. The only thing I love more than playing tennis is watching really talented professional tennis players compete.

On September 11, 1999, I was in the stands on a hot Saturday afternoon, watching Andre Agassi play an epic five-set match against Yevgeny Kafelnikov in the men's semifinal. Both players were on fire, and neither would cede a point without chasing down every lob or launching killer backhands down the line.

I was not just there to enjoy world-class tennis that day. I was there to try to steal Andre away from NBC. I had done a profile on him for *GMA* two months earlier—it was an extraordinary story. Once ranked number 1 in the world, he dropped all the way down to number 141, before fighting his way back up. If he won this tournament, he would win back his number 1 ranking. *GMA* wanted him live on our show Monday morning. My producers were hoping I might convince him to skip the *Today* show live interview that had been scheduled and do ours instead.

Andre beat Kafelnikov—he was on his way to the finals. I waited for him in the USTA office. There were a handful of other people also there, waiting. Andre was doing press in the other room; this was taking a long time. I was starting to feel uncomfortable. *I should just leave*, I thought. *There is no way he is going to cancel* Today.

There were two men sitting on the couch, talking. One of Andre's team walked in and gave them each a big hug. "Man, you were amazing last night! You really put Andre in the right head space. It meant so much to him."

Despite my discomfort, I was curious. Who were these guys? What did they do last night?

Then, just as I was about to gather my purse and leave a note with Andre's manager, one of the men turned to me. "Are you here to do a story on Andre?"

"No." I shook my head. "I already did one. I am just here to congratulate him, and invite him onto our show." I couldn't help myself, I had to ask. "What did you do for him last night?"

"We put on a private concert for him."

"How cool! What did you play?"

"A few songs off one of my records."

I was intrigued. "What is your name?"

"Marc Cohn."

I hesitated. His friend jumped in.

"You probably know him from his first hit, 'Walking in Memphis.'"

"Oh yes…" I said. "But I actually preferred your second album, *The Rainy Season*. It's brilliant." It had been one of my favorite CDs six years earlier. I had played it over and over, and still knew almost every lyric by heart. I especially loved the song "Medicine Man." It was haunting, his voice husky.

At that moment, Andre emerged from the locker room, elated with his hard-won victory. We all exchanged hugs and talked for a while. Marc was planning to come back to watch the finals on Sunday. Andre turned to me, "Why don't you come? I will give you one of my seats."

I was thrilled to be invited, happy to say yes. Marc and I made plans to go to the final the next day together, where we watched Andre win the championship and reclaim his ranking at the top of the tennis world.

The next day, Monday, Marc left a message on my voice mail, inviting me to dinner because he would like to discuss a story idea. I burst out laughing. That has got to be the most transparent line ever used on a journalist. I knew exactly what he was doing—he was asking me out on a date.

We made arrangements to go to dinner Wednesday night to a fantastic Italian restaurant on the Upper East Side. But when I woke up that morning, I didn't think we'd make it. A vicious storm was rolling toward the city, with torrential rains and severe flooding on the way. The streets crossing Central Park were closed because of high water. The mayor was on TV warning New Yorkers to stay home that night. In all my time living in this city, I cannot remember another time when Manhattan has shut down for a thunderstorm.

Marc and I were undeterred. He picked me up, we found a cab, and somehow we made our way through the lashing rain to Scalinatella. My friends Dana, Michelle, and Lori and I had come here often. I knew the menu by heart. The place was always packed, with people waiting on the stairs for a precious table. Not this night. The restaurant was nearly empty. Marc and I had our pick of cozy tables. It was a wonderful night. As the wind howled outside, we told each other about our lives. I learned how he fell in love with music, that as a boy he loved the same song I did, "Angel of the Morning," by Merrilee Rush. He told me how he was writing music by the time he was twelve, and playing in bands in his teens. He told me about the night he won a Grammy for Best New Artist. He told me about his divorce, and his two young children, and how painful that was. And I told him everything about me...everything except the anxiety. But I would eventually tell him, and only him, about how much I struggled with it.

We sipped wine and shared pasta and nibbled on fish,

marveling at the stormy weather that September night. We laughed. "Could it be an omen?" Could it?

After that night, our first date, I never went out with anyone else. I never kissed anyone else. For me, there was just Marc.

—⁂—

A Happy Time

After a year or so of seriously dating Marc, our relationship moved to the next step. He was the first person I had ever trusted enough to confide in about my anxiety and insecurity. He was soulful, smart, romantic, deep. He would sing me to sleep when I could not calm myself. We spent hours talking over dinners I cooked for him at my apartment; he would later tell people, "I fell in love with her at that dining room table!" The first time I saw him perform in concert I was so nervous and felt so protective of him—afraid the audience would not give him the respect he was due. He was halfway through the first song before I realized *He's got this!* He was, and is, masterful on stage. He owns it. And that night I could see he had every single member of the audience in his hand. I felt incredibly proud. I loved hearing about his music, and other music he loved. He introduced me to Daniel Lanois and Mavis Staples (musically) and Bonnie Raitt and Jackson Browne (literally). For the first time in my life, I felt safe. He took care of me.

I remember flying home from Sydney, Australia, in the

wee hours of New Year's Day 2000. I had been part of ABC's millennial extravaganza. Peter Jennings anchored for twenty-four hours straight, with anchors and correspondents around the globe in every time zone. I was the first to herald in the new century from my post in front of the Sydney Opera House, where it was freezing and raining. By the time I boarded my flight back to the United States a short time later, the cold I had been nursing had blossomed into bronchitis. My ears were so plugged up I could barely hear. I called Marc from the plane in tears. He soothed me and told me of an old singers' trick where you put a warm, wet paper towel in a plastic cup and hold the cup around your ear. It worked, and I listened on the airplane phone (yes, they still had them then!) as he described the fireworks over New York City that night.

By New Year's Eve 2001 we were talking about getting married. He had just been through a bruising seven-year divorce that lasted longer than the marriage, with two young children, so there was a lot to consider. Even so, one night that spring I came home, still in my sweats from the quick visit to the gym after work, and he greeted me on one knee in my apartment and proposed. I still remember how his hand shook as he held out the beautiful diamond ring he had picked out on his own. Laughing, crying, in shock, I said yes! He had thought of everything: a bouquet of roses awaited on the table, a bottle of Champagne sat on ice, and he proceeded to serve me a meal from my favorite restaurant, Nobu. "I can't believe this!" I kept repeating, over and over. "I have to call my parents!" I exclaimed.

"I've already asked your father for your hand, and we have his blessing," he said. It touched me deeply that he had shown my family such respect. I knew how much it meant to them.

As soon as we got engaged, we began trying to have a baby. This was very important to me—I was thirty-nine. I had never been pregnant, and I didn't know if I could even conceive. We set a wedding date for October.

We wanted something small and elegant, less than a hundred guests, black tie, a live band (a must when the groom is a Grammy award–winning singer!), and a sit-down dinner. I began shopping for wedding dresses and was quickly at a loss. I had no clue what I wanted to wear. I had never looked at a bridal magazine in my life. A couple visits to bridal boutiques left me baffled— the lovely salesclerks and their questions—"What are you looking for? Something with ruffles? Crystals on the bodice? Long sleeves?" It was only after wandering into Vera Wang's boutique on Madison Avenue that I found the perfect choice: a strapless raw silk dress, pale ivory, with a velvet sash around the waist. Simple. Elegant. I loved it the moment I put it on.

And then exactly one week after I ordered the dress, I found out I was pregnant. I was thrilled. Part of me could not believe it—even though I had wanted it so badly, and we had been trying so hard, it was still a miracle to me.

Marc and I called my mom and dad first, and I started crying—tears of joy. My mom cried, too. "Oh, honey, we are so thrilled for you. We were worried this might not happen for you!" My dad was jubilant, and laughed. "What have the two of you been doing?" I just remember crying and laughing on the phone—so happy to tell them, a tiny bit relieved that my very Catholic parents didn't disapprove since we had not yet walked down the aisle.

There was no way my newly ordered Vera Wang gown would still fit me in October, so we moved the date up to July 22, when I would be just shy of three months along. We told no one about the baby on the way except family, but some friends and colleagues told me later they guessed I was pregnant when it seems overnight I morphed from a B cup to something akin to Dolly Parton proportions. That, and the fact that I had stopped drinking. I was so nauseous those first few months, it should have been easier than it was to give it up. But it wasn't. I missed drinking wine at night, even when I felt green around the gills. By this time, I had already moderated my drinking significantly. Marc had insisted on it, before agreeing to try to start a family.

He had first called me on my drinking one evening about a year after we began dating. We had been out to dinner at a restaurant, where I had consumed several glasses of wine while he sipped his customary Scotch. We returned to his apartment, where he poured two small glasses of Remy (his favorite nightcap) for each of us. Too small, it turned out, for me. I helped myself to another, at which point he said, "I think maybe you've had enough."

"Are you kidding?" I was shocked. Furious. Really furious. No one had ever said that to me before.

He persisted. "I think you drink too much." I now understand that he was legitimately concerned, but back then I lashed out: "Me? A drinking problem?"

I was speechless. I stood up, put on my coat, and walked out. Marc ran after me and grabbed my arm. "Elizabeth, you have a problem with alcohol." But I didn't want to hear about it, although deep inside, some part of me must have recognized it was true.

Although Marc's remark hit me like a slap in the face, eventually I came to understand and agree—not wholeheartedly enough to swear off drinking, but sufficiently to start to moderate my alcohol consumption. In the beginning it was hard, very hard. That should have been a tip-off to my growing dependency. But at that point I was able to cut way back. I wanted to be with Marc, and I wanted to have a baby. For several years early in the marriage, Marc would remark, often with admiration, at how well I had gotten my drinking under control. And for a while, I suppose I had.

I loved being married. For the first time in my life I didn't feel alone. I belonged to someone, and he belonged to me. I remember one evening walking into our apartment together, just two months before our firstborn would arrive, suddenly being struck by a thought. "Just think," I said to Marc, "soon we will never again walk into an empty apartment. Our baby will be here. I can't even imagine that."

Marc answered, "One day you won't even remember what it's like to walk into an empty dark apartment." Never in my toughest moments, or in the hard times to come, did I ever think I would once again open my front door to a dark and vacant home. Looking back, there were warning signs—tiny fissures that would grow and drive us far apart—but we didn't heed them. The fault lines that would later swallow us up were buried under the whirlwind of our newly wedded life: buying an apartment, moving in with Marc, becoming a stepmother, awaiting the day I would finally give birth to our first child.

In January 2003 I woke up every single morning and wondered, will this be the day? As the due date loomed, and then passed, it seemed our baby would never come. I had what is known in medical terms as a failure to progress: the baby hadn't begun to drop and I didn't dilate. Two weeks after my due date, my doctor decided to induce. I was admitted, and we waited...and waited...and waited. It was Friday evening, and I remember watching *World News Tonight* on the hospital monitor when a sick feeling washed over me...so powerful I could not even turn my head to tell Marc something was wrong.

One of the nurses monitoring my vital signs at the main desk ran into the room and pushed Marc aside. "I am going to push this button—it's an alarm. Get ready!" Suddenly, after hours of inertia, there was a frenzy of activity. Doctors were running. An orderly was racing me down a hall to an operating room. Marc was whisked off to change into surgical scrubs. And I still couldn't speak. I had spiked a fever of 105 degrees. The baby's heart rate had dropped. My doctor shouted to me, through my delirium, "Elizabeth, we have to get him out now. We're going to do a cesarean."

As I lay on the table in the middle of the crowded operating room I could hear all the voices—the doctors, the nurses, the anesthesiologist—but it was as though they were far away. I was shaking and cold, and kept trying to hug my arms to myself to get warm. "Lie still!" someone yelled. There was an IV in my arm. I was going to knock it loose if I kept moving. Seconds later, delirious from fever and fatigue, I forgot and tried again to wrap my arms close. It was just a matter of minutes before my doctor lifted my beautiful boy high in the air for me to see. "Oh, Elizabeth," she said. "He looks just like you!"

It was dramatic, and scary, and I was terribly sick, but that day, January 31, 2003, was one of the two best days of my life.

*   *   *

I took eleven weeks off of work to stay with my precious new baby. That was all of the time I could take with pay—nine weeks of paid maternity leave and two weeks of vacation time that I had saved up for this. We could not afford to be without my salary, even for a few weeks (tiny fissure, growing). Marc's financial obligations to his ex-wife meant I was the sole supporter of our family.

I savored every day of those eleven weeks. Zachary was an easy baby—he slept well and nursed easily. I loved nursing. I loved looking down at him in wonder. I still could not believe he was real. I would sit in my bed with him propped up on my knees and just stare at him. He looked like an angel. But too soon, I had to go back to work. I was determined to nurse as long as I could, so I carried a breast pump built into a backpack and empty bottles with me every day to the office. I had bought the contraption at a little shop called the Upper Breast Side (yes, that really is the name), and while I detested pumping—the wheezing and chugging of the machine and the tubes that made me feel like Elsie the Cow—I loved nursing so much I was willing to do it.

Even though I would have liked more time to be at home, I loved my job and was happy to be back at it, now as the co-host of *20/20*. The already legendary Barbara Walters had decided to retire...sort of. She was at the helm of the talk show she founded, *The View*, and still contributed specials to *20/20*. It was at times awkward, sort of like being on a stage with an icon enjoying her standing ovation...while waiting in the wings, unsure when it was appropriate to tiptoe into the spotlight.

It was a big promotion, and it allowed me more of the in-depth, long-form reporting that I loved. *20/20* gave me a huge platform to do meaningful stories. In the many years I have had this job, I have traveled the world. We traveled to Cambodia to do a story on baby trafficking. I went to the orphanages in Phnom Penh, teeming with babies and toddlers, desperate to be held. As we drove out of the city to remote villages, our car swerved around dozens of bicycles with entire families loaded on them—children perched on handlebars, mothers with infants slung around their chests on the seat behind a father, standing and pedaling. I had to cover my eyes I was so terrified one of the many cars speeding along would hit them. Once we arrived in the village, I interviewed a young mother who had sold her baby girl to the orphanage for 15 dollars. She told us she could not feed her baby, and had been promised the baby would be returned once she had the resources to care for her. She did not know that her baby had already been adopted by an American family who had been misled—told their little girl had no mother. The American woman arranging the adoptions went to prison after our report aired.

I remember covering the horrifying story of the murder of Lacy Peterson—a beautiful young woman in the bay area, eight months pregnant with her first child. As suspicion turned on her husband, now convicted of killing her, I wondered how many other pregnant women had disappeared, without all the media frenzy and attention. My team and I found the stories of four other women in the Bay Area also pregnant, who also vanished without a trace. There was no national media camped out in their front yards. They were all black or Hispanic. So I did an hour report about them, and why their stories were ignored while Lacy Peterson's was not. The expert on media that I interviewed pointed out Lacy had vanished during the Christmas holiday—generally a slow news cycle. Her family also immediately went on television to plead for the public's help, guaranteeing coverage. Our expert also pointed out the harsh reality that Lacy was pretty, and well-off, and came from a nice neighborhood. Most inescapably, Lacy was white. I was very proud to tell the stories of those other four women, who were from poorer communities, and were people of color, and whose lives were just as important.

In addition to my new job as co-host of *20/20* I was asked to fill in more regularly for Peter Jennings. The higher-ups trusted me with the crown jewel of the whole division. It was an exhilarating work/life juggling act; millions of working mothers know how difficult it can be. I soon slipped back into sipping a nightly glass of wine... or two...to take the edge off the day.

I wasn't particularly trying to hide anxiety or bury

unwanted feelings. I just wanted to unwind, which I began to do the second I walked into the apartment and poured myself a glass of chardonnay. Looking back, it seemed innocuous. I knew a lot of people who had a couple drinks at night to relax. Marc and I laughed a few years later when Zachary called my nightly glass of wine "mommy's juice." We thought it was cute. I wasn't drinking to excess, and I never woke up regretting what I had consumed the night before or feeling its effects. But it was a pattern of behavior that set me on a dangerous path.

—⚹—

Fault Lines

It's April 5, 2005, shortly before six p.m. Peter Jennings is in the studio trying to pre-tape a short personal message to the viewers. He's having a hard time. His voice is hoarse and he struggles to speak. He is gaunt; worry lines etch his face. I am in my office, having been urgently summoned the day before from a shoot in Hawaii and told I was needed immediately in New York. Something is up, but until a few hours ago, I didn't know much beyond the fact that it was deeply troubling and had shaken the upper echelon of the network. Now the world would learn the terrible news.

I sit behind my desk, watching the inner network feed with my senior producer, Terri Lichstein. Time slows down in that frightening way that it does when you see an oncoming car before you collide with it. My heart sinks. Terri's face is frozen in shock.

After trying and failing to record his message to the millions of people who tune into him every night, Peter tries once more.

"Finally, this evening, a brief note about change. Some

of you have noticed in the last several days that I was not covering the pope. While my colleagues at ABC did a superb job, I did think a few times that I was missing out; however, as some of you now know, I have learned in the last couple of days that I have lung cancer. Yes, I was a smoker until about twenty years ago, and I was weak and I smoked over 9/11. But whatever the reason, the news does slow you down a bit. I've been reminding my colleagues today that almost ten million Americans are already living with cancer, and I have a lot to learn from them. And *living* is the key word. The National Cancer Institute says that we are survivors from the moment of diagnosis."

It seems there isn't a sound in the hallways of ABC as we all watch Peter glance down and take a breath.

"I will continue to do the broadcast. On good days my voice will not always be like this."

He smiles. My heart breaks for him.

"Certainly it's been a long time, and I hope it goes without saying that a journalist who doesn't value the audience's loyalty should be in another line of work. To be perfectly honest, I'm surprised at the kindness of so many people. That's not intended to be false modesty, but even I was taken aback at how far and how fast news travels. Finally, I wonder if other men and women ask their doctors right away, 'Okay, Doc, when does the hair go?'"

Peter chuckles, and then tilts his head slightly to the side.

"At any rate, that's it for now on *World News Tonight*. I'm Peter Jennings. Thanks and good night."

Terri turns to me, her eyes huge, and we stare at each other. "Oh my God," she whispers. Just then my phone rings. It's Paul Slavin, the executive producer of *World News Tonight*. "Come down to the newsroom right away. We need you to anchor tonight's news."

I throw on a dress and blazer I keep hanging on the back of my door and run through the connecting corridor to the newsroom, where I'm shown the scripts and briefed on the reporting for the broadcast—at this point, just forty minutes to air. "Now go into hair and makeup!"

As I make my way to hair and makeup, I see Peter sitting quietly in his office with a few producers. I tap on the door: "I'm so sorry, Peter."

He looks up, smiles—this is so like the Peter Jennings we all respect and love so much—and then he apologizes for giving me such short notice. "I'm sorry to do this to you. Thank you for helping out."

I stammer, "It's okay. I am happy to. Anything I can do for you, just let me know."

I linger for a moment longer in his doorway, and then run upstairs to the set.

I didn't know it then, but that would be the last time I would ever see Peter. He would go on to wage a coura-geous battle against cancer for four and a half months, one I believed he would win until the day he didn't. On the set that night in April, I breathed in to calm my nerves, anchored the newscast, and, at the end, introduced the message he had taped for his loyal viewers. It would be the last time they, too, saw the man they had trusted every night, on the air. The following week, Charlie Gibson and I began to share the evening news duties. We both kept our "real" jobs—he as co-host of *Good Morning America*; I as co-anchor of *20/20*. The two of us worked hard to keep the ship afloat, so to speak. The news division was badly shaken by Peter's cancer. The uncertainty was rampant, along with the worried questions, whispered in hallways. How long would Peter be gone? Would he ever come back? Could he survive? Peter Jennings was the face of ABC News, and now suddenly he was gone. Charlie and I both knew it was vital to be steady and consistent, and to never forget whose chair we filled every night at 6:30. We each ended every broadcast by saying "For Peter Jennings, and all of us at ABC News, good night."

As I filled in anchoring the evening news week after week, I never told anyone how nervous I would get as show time approached. I was afraid if I did, the response would be "Oh, we made a terrible mistake putting you in this anchor chair. You don't belong there!" The years of hearing from one local news director after another that I couldn't make it as an anchor, combined with my own innate insecurity, led me to protect my secret anxiety at all costs. The only people who knew were my parents and Marc.

As airtime approached each day, my anxiety would build. At five p.m., ninety minutes before air, I would nibble on pretzels so I had something in my stomach—but not too much. At five thirty, I would call Marc and whisper into the phone that I was nervous, and he would soothe me. "You are going to be great, just like every other night. Relax." At six, I would get up and walk down the hallway, away from the rim, which was humming with activity at thirty minutes to air. As I walked away from everyone for a moment I would stretch my arms high up, my finger-tips reaching for the ceiling, and take deep breaths to slow my pounding heart. And in the moments before the show started, while sitting at the anchor desk, microphone on my chest, IFB in my ear, I would close my eyes briefly and urge myself to be calm. "Slow down," I would whisper. (I always start to talk too fast when I am nervous.) "Think about what you are about to say. Focus on these stories of tragedy, bravery, feats of humanity, and survival that you are about to tell. Stay in the moment. Don't think about the millions of people watching. Don't worry about how a small stumble in the good evening page will undermine your credibility. Focus on these amazing stories—that is what is important. Focus. Breathe."

The memory of that horrible night—years ago—in Chicago when I had a panic attack on air was always with me. But it never happened again, and as I anchored week after week, sharing the duties with Charlie, the anxiety began to subside. It never disappeared, but I grew to manage it.

For the next few months, I traded off with Charlie Gibson as the anchor of *World News Tonight* for two, sometimes three days per week. I was the only woman anchoring a network evening newscast and the first Latina. Then, as now, it was the domain of men.

But I was not just the only woman at that point; I was the only anchor who was also the parent of a young child. Zachary was just two, and I desperately wanted to be the best mother possible. For five months I juggled it all—my job as co-host of *20/20* and reporting the in-depth stories on that show, anchoring *World News Tonight*, and racing to preschool for pickups and parent groups and play dates.

I was honored that ABC trusted me to fill in for Peter. About halfway through that time, I found out I was pregnant again. I was thrilled—Marc and I had been hoping to have another baby. I was incredibly excited. I didn't tell anyone except my parents and my sister; no one at work knew. Because I was forty-two, my doctor was monitoring my hormone levels carefully. Then one morning she called to say something was wrong. The levels were off; I needed to go in for an ultrasound. The specialist she sent me to see was lovely and kind. But she was very quiet as she studied the black-and-white images on the screen.

"We can't find the embryo. It's either ectopic or you have lost it."

I was stunned. "What do you mean you can't find it? I don't understand." Tears filled my eyes.

The doctor gave me a gentle smile. "This happens sometimes. We need you to come in every morning for the next week for blood tests. We will know more in a few days."

I left the doctor's office in a daze. And when, five days later, she called to tell me I had in fact lost the baby, I could not believe the depths of my grief. I closed my office door and called my mother and sobbed. She, too, had suffered a miscarriage, and she understood how profoundly sad I felt. In just two months I had, to my surprise, developed a deep emotional connection to that life inside me—a life I would never know. After crying for quite some time on the phone with my mom, I dried my eyes, took a deep breath, opened the door, and went back to work. Just as I had not told anyone at work that I was pregnant, I told no one I had miscarried.

By late July, it was becoming clear inside ABC that Peter might not win his battle against cancer. No one ever said that. On the contrary, we all continued to speak about him as if he would come back, even when our words rang hollow. It was as if we could will him to get better, walk back through the door, and take the helm again, if we just stayed stubbornly optimistic.

Then came August 7, 2005…a day seared in my memory. Marc was on tour out west. He had been out of town for several days, so I had a babysitter sleeping over at the house to help out on the days I was working. After rocking Zachary to sleep, I went to bed. We had been getting phone calls in the middle of the night for the past few months from an unknown fax line, so I switched off the ringer on the phone. I was awakened hours later, early the next morning, by the doorman from our building pounding on my front door. ABC News had been trying to reach me—and so had my husband's tour manager. Their phone calls had been muted, all night long, as they tried to deliver terrible news: During the night Peter Jennings had died. But even more shocking, my husband had been shot! Marc and his band had just finished a concert in downtown Denver and were on their way in a van back to the hotel when someone attempted to carjack them. A man, high on drugs, had pulled a gun, aimed straight at the van, and fired.

"Elizabeth, Marc has been shot." Shane Fontayne's voice was shaky on the phone. He was more than Marc's guitarist; he was a close friend.

"What? What?" I couldn't process what he was saying. I was still half asleep. I actually wondered if I was still asleep and having a terrible dream.

"What do you mean he's been shot? Is he okay?"

"He's okay. We are at the emergency room now. The doctors are with him."

"Where was he shot? What happened?" Adrenaline was kicking in. I knew then that it was no dream.

Shane hesitated a beat. "He was shot in the head. But he's okay."

In the head??? That's not possible. I could not make sense of it. How could Marc be shot? How on earth could he be shot in the head and be okay? The rest of that early morning was a blur. I called the airline and got a seat on the next flight to Denver. In between packing a bag and making arrangements with the nanny, I finally spoke to Marc, who sounded shaky and so scared. He told me that moments before the attack, sitting in the van, he had seen a man running a block ahead. He remembered thinking, *I wonder what he is running from?*—not knowing that the man was running from a crazed drug addict with a gun, and that moments later that addict would open fire on them. The bullet punctured the window and ricocheted off the steering wheel and one of the doors before it struck Marc, lodging right below his temple.

He was freakishly lucky—it was terrifying, but he was alive and physically all right. When I arrived in Denver later that day, Marc had been discharged from the emergency room and was back at the hotel. I helped him change the dressing on the wound, trying not to flinch when I saw the small, deep hole just above his cheekbone. We flew back to New York the next day, his tour cut short. I was focused on his physical injury...deeply relieved he was okay. But I missed the deeper wound, the one that shook him to the core, the one he needed me to see. I was too quick to marvel at Marc's good fortune, too anxious to get home to Zachary, too consumed with the tragedy of Peter's death and the deep sadness in the hallways of ABC.

I returned to work, where the pall of Peter's passing hung over Sixty-sixth Street. The entire news division was in shock at the loss of its leader, uncertain of what the future would hold. Peter had been more than the face of ABC News, he had been its leader. He had led us through 9/11, through the start of a long war in Iraq, through presidential elections, through decades of crises, tragedies, and world events. His death left an enormous void for everyone. And enormous uncertainty. What would happen next? For the next four and a half months Charlie and I did our best to carry on, because...well, what else could we do? The world did not stop—the war in the Middle East, Hurricane Katrina, the tsunami in southeast Asia sweeping away hundreds of thousands of lives. An audience of 25 million still learned about these stories that affected their world from the evening newscasts on the three main networks—ABC, NBC, and CBS.

That's a lot of human beings, but, at the same time, viewership was eroding. New digital platforms were already beginning to sound the death knell for magazines and newspapers. The Internet and cable were luring more and more viewers away from traditional news. Changes were afoot at ABC. David Westin, the president of ABC

News, decided to shake things up. He wanted to go for a younger audience in an attempt to counterbalance the graying of the bulk of evening news viewers. His solution was daring and ambitious: to have two anchors; one in the field and one in the studio, covering breaking news. His plan was to pair me with Bob Woodruff, a well-respected, experienced reporter at ABC. Westin offered Bob and me new contracts to start the job immediately.

It was a bold plan, and it was dramatically different from the other two network newscasts. We would also be live every night for the West Coast broadcasts, updating news for the millions of viewers three hours later. But I hesitated. I had enjoyed anchoring when I was recruited during Peter's illness and death, but it was never a job that I ever wanted as my own. I felt I was more suited to the evening news magazine work on *20/20*, with its in-depth features and the give-and-take of interviews. I felt more comfortable anchoring the morning show, with its less scripted, more relaxed vibe, and where you could ad-lib.

Anchoring the evening news is more constricting. Everything has to fit into tightly plotted blocks, timed and scripted down to the second. And I worried that the demanding schedule of one of us on the road and live until ten p.m. every night would be a challenge for my family. How would this affect my young son, I wondered? My marriage? I stalled, trying to decide.

I was on a shoot in New Orleans for *20/20* when David Westin called to tell me Bob had signed the deal. They were waiting on me. And still, I worried…a small voice inside me telling me this new plan was too ambitious, this new live, traveling newscast would exact too high a toll on my young family.

"Elizabeth." Westin's voice came through my phone, reassuring me. "This is a good thing."

I told him I needed the weekend to think about it, and then called Sunday night to say I would do it, but only if I could continue on as co-host of *20/20*. I was worried, honestly, that this would not work out. "Great!" he said. "We need you to sign the contract at seven thirty tomorrow morning, in my office." *What's the rush?* I thought. *Wouldn't nine a.m. do?*

What I didn't know was that the network had set up a press conference announcing the anchor change, and that right after signing the deal, I would be sitting with David Westin and Bob Woodruff, fielding questions about the new arrangement that I was still asking myself. How would this work? Why are we the best people at the network to anchor this show? Why didn't ABC go with someone more experienced (like Charlie)? How do you decide when to travel and where to travel? Is this a stunt?

The next few weeks were a whirlwind. Bob was a seasoned reporter (as well as one of the most decent people I have ever had the privilege to work with), and we began learning the dance of co-anchoring together. After my initial trepidation, I was beginning to feel excited about this new opportunity. I would sit next to Bob, night after night, and marvel that he seemed to feel none of the nerves or anxiety with which I still secretly struggled. He seemed to need none of the preshow calming routines in which I still indulged. Because I was now anchoring five nights a week, the fear of an on-air panic attack receded a bit. But it was still there.

Just two weeks into our new arrangement, ABC wanted to send me to Iraq to cover the first free elections since Saddam Hussein had fallen. Peter had gone to Iraq many times, as had Bob. Coming, as I did, from the news magazine world of *20/20* (with its longer features and personal profiles), my bosses wanted to establish my hard news credentials.

They didn't flat-out order me to Iraq. Instead they let me mull it over and come to the conclusion that I ought to go. In contrast to the free-form anxiety that is always present in some way for me, going to Iraq was different. I was scared. This fear was sharp and defined: I was afraid to go into a war zone. Afraid I would be hurt or killed. Afraid I would leave my two-year-old son without a mother. Marc said the decision on whether to go was up to me, and eventually, I responded to ABC's request like the daughter of a soldier. I agreed to go, packing my fear along with my khaki pants and desert boots. Bob's wife, Lee, called Marc to reassure him that I would be okay. She had been in his position during Bob's many trips to Iraq. She understood what it meant to see your spouse head off to a dangerous place.

To add to the tension, the night before I left, I had the unmistakable feeling that I was pregnant, so I ran out and bought a home pregnancy test. Sure enough, my suspicions were confirmed. It was very early in the process—I was at most just a couple weeks along—but there was no question about it. Still, since I wasn't far along at all, I resolved to go ahead with the trip.

I called my sister, Aimie, and my mom from the airport on my way to the Middle East: "If something happens to me," I said, "I want someone to know I was pregnant." I told no one else, not even Marc. I was afraid he would tell me not to go, and that he would not trust that this was still the right thing for me to do.

So I was off to Baghdad, where our plane descended over the Iraqi capital at a steep angle, executing a cork-screw maneuver, which makes the plane harder to hit with a shoulder-mounted surface-to-air missile. When I cleared customs, my security detail met me. I suppose I was expecting two pumped-up guys, big as NFL fullbacks, with brush cuts and sunglasses. Instead, two nondescript men materialized and without breaking stride came up alongside me as I walked and said, "Elizabeth, we are from Pilgrim Security, and we will be with you during your trip."

Despite their unassuming appearance, I could not have been in better hands during my week of anchoring from that tortured and devastated land. All the Pilgrims, as everyone called them, are highly trained armed forces veterans, often British, Australian, or South African. They provide security all over the world, wherever violence, kidnappings, and assassinations are serious hazards. Rather than calling attention to themselves, they are highly skilled at melting into the background. But unobtrusive should not be confused with unprepared. They were armed to the teeth and very, very good at what they do. While we walked to the car they took my bags and slipped a bulletproof vest on me. One of them, a Brit, introduced himself. "I will be with you wherever you go. You don't go anywhere unless I am at your side." He had red hair—which earned him the nickname Ginger. I decided at that moment not to worry about being safe—they would do that. That was their job—I would focus on doing mine.

We walked through the parking lot, stopping finally in front of a beat-up-looking car. "This is what we are driving in?" I asked, surprised.

"It's important we blend in, don't attract attention to ourselves," they explained as we piled in.

The doors were heavy—it took all my strength to open one.

"Armored," Ginger said, observing my struggle.

Once inside they explained that the windows do not open; they are bulletproof. Wedged in the backseat in my vest, with a Pilgrim on either side, we set off on the treacherous Airport Road leading into the heart of

Baghdad. That route was infamous for the number of attacks along it—every diplomat, journalist, and contractor had to travel it—lots of tantalizing targets for terrorists. There were improvised explosive devices (IEDs) detonating with regularity, and ambush attacks from alongside the road. We wove our way around the huge holes that had been blasted in the pavement, and threaded the concrete barriers erected to provide some modicum of safety, and made our way to the ABC bureau.

I spent the first half of the trip based in Baghdad, shooting stories around the city during the day, then staying up to co-anchor ABC's evening newscast at two a.m. Iraq time. I did whatever the Pilgrims ordered me to do, immediately. One time I was shooting interviews with Iraqis in an open-air market. I was mid-question when Ginger put his hand on my shoulder and said, "We are leaving now." I did exactly as he ordered... thanked the man I was interviewing and walked quickly away. I have no idea what he saw that unnerved him, but I wasn't about to wait and ask.

There was just one truly hairy situation, though (at least the only one I was aware of). We were driving from Baghdad to Camp Victory, a huge army base outside the city where we would rebase for the next few days. Trying to avoid driving along Airport Road again, we found ourselves in a warren of small streets in a neighborhood dense with houses and huge pools of sewage in the street. We must have taken a wrong turn, because we kept turning onto streets that led into dead ends. Our caravan of three beat-up armored cars circled the streets slowly, looking for the way out of this labyrinth. We were the only Westerners in sight, and Iraqis were beginning to emerge from their homes to stare. The Pilgrims were tense, on edge, quite the opposite of their normal cool demeanor. The two in my car disagreed on our next move. One of them wanted to get out of the car and suss out the situation, get directions to the nearest way out. The other disagreed: "No way. If you get out I can't cover you" (as in "back you up with my gun"). A member of our ABC crew sitting next to me started to freak out. It took nearly half an hour, but we finally picked our way through the maze and found the road to Camp Victory.

When we arrived, we set up our editing stations and satellite feeds in one of Saddam Hussein's former palaces. It was made entirely of marble: walls, ceilings, floors. As the only woman on the trip I had my own bedroom, while all the men shared the other two. While the marble was beautiful, it was absolutely freezing. There was little, if any, heat, and the marble retained none of it. I don't think I have ever been so cold in my entire life. One night, after anchoring the news, jumping up and down in place to get warm when I was off camera, I put on every single article of clothing in my suitcase to go to sleep. I still couldn't get warm.

On the historic day when the first free elections were held (how hopeful we were before the country fell apart again!), I flew around Baghdad with General William Webster, visiting polling places where Iraqis had lined up for hours waiting their turn to vote and then dip their fingers in ink to keep anyone from voting twice. This was not as simple as a helicopter sightseeing trip over New York Harbor. Apart from the hazards of ground fire and shoulder-launched missiles, we had to contend with severe turbulence and sudden dust storms. At times, we'd be making good progress and then drop like a stone when we hit an air pocket. At one of the polling places we visited, General Webster's soldiers were working with Iraqi troops, enforcing security.

It was near lunchtime. The Iraqi general in charge said to General Webster and my crew, "It would be my honor if you would join me to lunch."

It was a gracious invitation, but remember, I was pregnant—that is, somewhere between not hungry and nauseous most of the time. Add to this the fact that we had been warned about not drinking or even brushing our teeth using local water. General Webster diplomatically agreed to the lunch and we all trooped into the Iraqi leader's conference room. I warily eyed the large table in the middle, laden with food, smiled, and said, "No, thank you," as one of the Iraqis handed me a plate. "Take it," my producer whispered in my ear. "It will be insulting to them if you don't. Just pretend to eat."

So I served myself and proceeded to do a pantomime of eating and enjoying. I thanked our Iraqi hosts, who were clearly honored to be hosting an American general and a network television crew. I was so convincing at pretending to devour my meal that as we left, one of General Webster's men said to me, "Oh, ma'am, you're going to be awfully sick after eating that."

I smiled and said, "Don't worry. I didn't actually eat a bite!"

I found out later that General Webster and his men all carried Cipro (an antibiotic) with them to guard against a variety of things, including getting sick from eating or drinking anything from a part of the world to which our stomachs were not accustomed.

That week was long and exhausting, but ultimately exhilarating. We did stories on the elections, on the dubious fitness of Iraqi troops, on the diplomatic battles raging in the Green Zone, and on the fight for control over the future of Iraq. But the story that earned me the most audience reaction was one I did on the Baghdad ballet school—a place that had been firebombed, but where little boys and girls showed up anyway to learn to dance the *Nutcracker* while armed guards stood at the door. That week in Iraq was the most rewarding of my career. I got a lovely note from Bob Woodruff as I anchored my final broadcast that week from Baghdad. "I am honored to have you as my co-anchor," he wrote. It meant the world to me.

When I returned to New York, the whirlwind

continued unabated. I got off the plane from Amman and went straight to the studio to anchor a special report with Bob on Iraq. We flew to the West Coast to promote our new concept of the evening news. One of us was almost always on an airplane to anchor the evening broadcast live from a news event in the field. Despite my initial trepidation, in those first weeks working with Bob I was beginning to enjoy myself, and I began to think, *Maybe, just maybe, this will work.*

Drinking wasn't a problem for me then. I was a few weeks pregnant and so queasy I wasn't even tempted. As I anchored night after night, my lifelong nemesis, anxiety, subsided. I no longer feared that the smallest mistake on a given night would spell the end of my career. I began to feel more confident. And sharing the anchor desk with Bob meant I didn't feel quite so alone for that half hour of live television.

As President Bush's State of Union Address approached at the end of January, it was decided I would anchor our coverage from Washington and Bob would anchor from Iraq. On the day of the address, the president traditionally hosts a lunch at the White House with the anchors of the evening newscasts and the Sunday morning political shows. I was the only woman invited that year. I sat across from President Bush, and to my right was Vice President Dick Cheney. President Bush was personally warm, and passionate in defense of his policies. Everything said at the lunch is off the record, but each anchor at the table pressed the president for context and background information. It was absolutely fascinating. I kept reminding myself of the formality required in this elegant room, as we nibbled on the exquisite food. Next to me, the vice president was quiet for most of the meal. I noted he was the only one at the table who drank a glass of wine. (What do you want to bet I was the only anchor at that lunch who noticed that?)

I must have made some sort of impression because a few weeks after that lunch, we got a call from the White House that President Bush would sit down to do an interview with me. I arrived at the White House that day a bundle of nerves. I was actually shaking, I was so nervous as I waited to enter the Oval Office.

It was set up that the president would give me a tour as the cameras rolled. Before the interview we would walk from the Oval Office through the Rose Garden to the East Room, where the interview would take place. As I stood waiting, the door opened and one of the president's staffers said, "Ms. Vargas, the president would like to say hello before we start."

"Oh, okay," I stammered. I followed him into the Oval Office and instantly, my nervousness vanished. He was just a man, a human being. The president of the United States, yes, and the leader of the free world, of course. But maybe presidents get nervous too before doing national interviews. I don't know. At any rate, we laughed and exchanged some pleasantries, and then I turned to go back out to the waiting area.

"What's happening now?" he asked me.

"Well, Mr. President," I said, "I am going to leave and then come back in with the cameras rolling, as if this first greeting never took place!" Everything went smoothly, and the interview went a few minutes longer than our allotted twenty minutes. And when it was done, something extraordinary happened. President Bush leaned back in his chair, crossed his legs, and the two of us proceeded to talk for another fifteen minutes, as my producers crouched on the floor along the wall and the White House staffers huddled in the corner. No one moved. No one was going to interrupt him and say, "Um, Mr. President, it's time to go now," least of all me. I did not know then that usually the president—every president—is out of his chair and out the door before the anchor is finished saying thank you. For years, crew members in the Washington bureau told the story of that day. One of the president's advisors, who was there, Nicolle Wallace, told it again in 2015 on *The View*, when I appeared as a guest.

Our bold experiment, to devise a new, dynamic evening newscast, lasted one month. It was undone by profound violence on a road in Iraq, where Bob Woodruff was traveling one afternoon in late January in a tank.

He had flown to Iraq to report what was sure to be topic A of the president's State of the Union Address: the war that was consuming billions of American dollars and tens of thousands of American and Iraqi lives.

I vividly remember the day he left. We had done a joint interview with Howard Kurtz, who was then the media critic of the *Washington Post*. We posed together for a photo in front of our new set, Bob with a broad smile on his face. Then he gave me a bear hug and ran down the hall. "See you from Baghdad!" he called. I would not see him again for many, many months, and then he would be changed forever.

On January 29, 2006, I was awakened at five a.m. by the telephone. It is never good news when the phone rings that early, and that morning, the news was devastating. Paul Slavin, the executive vice president in charge of news, was on the line. He told me Bob and his crew had been in a convoy that had hit an IED. At the very moment of the explosion, Bob and his cameraman, Doug Vogt, had been standing with their heads and shoulders outside the tank shooting a stand up. Bob was wounded so seriously that medics on the scene weren't sure he would live.

Just as I had with Marc and his gunshot wound, I refused to believe the worst could happen. "Where is he now?" I asked. "Where was he hurt? Where is Lee?"—Lee Woodruff, Bob's wife, who had been so comforting to Marc when I was in Iraq a month earlier.

"Oh my God," I said to Marc as I hung up the phone. "Oh my God, we have to call Lee."

ABC was arranging to fly her to the Landstuhl army base in Germany, which has one of the best hospitals in the military. Bob was being flown there from Baghdad. When I reached Lee, shortly before her flight, I made guarantees I had no power to keep. "Bob is going to be fine. He is strong. It's going to be okay." It was as if I could will it into being so. If only.

Marc and I got up and dressed and gathered up Zachary and went to the office. Everyone was there. It was a Sunday morning. Zachary was clingy and feeling sick. He cried every time I put him down, so I sat with him on my lap, rocking him, as we all waited, hour after hour, for word on Bob's and Doug's conditions. As the updates trickled in from Iraq, each one seemed worse—Bob had suffered traumatic brain injury. Doug was gravely injured as well.

It would take days before we all learned how close Bob came to dying, and months to appreciate how miraculous his survival truly was. He was placed in an induced coma for thirty-six days to allow his brain to heal. Part of his skull was removed to relieve swelling. He fought valiantly to get better, and against all odds, he eventually did. But it would be more than a year before Bob could return to work at ABC News.

The immediate fallout from Bob's brush with death was that the curtain came down on ABC's unconventional two-anchor gambit, just twenty-seven days after it had officially begun. Once again, the news division was reeling, in crisis mode. David Westin's bold new idea was undone. He was back to square one, trying to figure out what to do. In those early days we were not sure how long it would take for Bob to recover, or how long I might be anchoring *World News Tonight* alone. I felt I had to be honest with David and tell him I was pregnant, even though I was still in my first trimester. I didn't think it was fair to allow him to make plans for the evening newscast without telling him I might be going on maternity leave in seven months. I called and asked for a meeting. When I arrived in his office, he looked drawn, worry lines creasing his face. I was nervous about telling him—afraid I was piling still more onto a platter of worry. But he was wonderful. He stood up, put his arms around me, gave me a comforting hug and said, "Congratulations. We could use some good news around here today!"

Not everyone in the news business was equally gracious. There were rumors that my pregnancy was the result of in vitro fertilization that I had been undergoing at the same time I was negotiating my new contract. It was all untrue. I had gotten pregnant naturally. But when the publicist for ABC came to my office to say that I had been seen the summer before in a doctor's office that specialized in fertility, I had to explain I was there because I had been pregnant then and had miscarried. The look on her face at that moment said so much—sympathy for my loss at that time, and discomfort at having to pry in order to shut down a rumor mill that could leak to the press.

Television news is a tough business, and it is brutally competitive. There were people in the news division who thought I was not up to anchoring *World News Tonight* by myself, but I was determined to succeed.

For the next several months, I worked extra hard, staying until ten p.m. three nights every week to do live updates for the West Coast. (When I was told I needed to stay all five nights until ten p.m., I did something I rarely did at ABC and said no, because it meant I would never see my son at all during the week.) I was doing my very best each day, even though I was green with nausea. The second pregnancy was harder—I felt sick the entire nine months, and much more exhausted.

The strain of my long hours at work was affecting my family. I felt guilt and anguish about missing important time with Zachary, who was now three and starting pre-school. Marc and I began arguing more over the time I spent working. The stress proved too much one day in my OB-GYN's office. Being pregnant meant lots of doctor visits to monitor my health and the baby's. But getting away from the office was difficult—I could not even leave the building to grab a sandwich or a coffee without telling my producers where I was going and how long I would be gone; someone would have to be camera-ready to cover for me in case of breaking news. These visits to see my doctor always involved a lot of waiting. One day, as I sat in the little examination room, my blue hospital gown stretched across my burgeoning tummy, I just lost it. I had been waiting for nearly an hour, checking my watch, growing more and more anxious by the minute. Finally, just as I was gathering my clothes to get dressed and leave, the doctor knocked on the door and walked in. I burst into tears, sobbing, telling her I could not take this kind of time off from work only to sit and wait, that I was feeling such enormous stress about proving myself and so guilty about taking this time off, that Marc was mad at me for working too much, that I was missing Zachary growing up—basically, everything. She was amazing. She apologized profusely for being so late, and listened sympathetically to everything. I just sat there and cried and cried. It was like a dam breaking for me. Then I dried my tears, put my clothes on, and went back to the office. I missed just one day of work during those months—the day of my amnio, and only then because doctors order women who have that test to go straight to bed for the rest of the day.

In spite of the long hours and the emotional burden on my home life, I began to enjoy the job. It's a rush to be part of a team, sifting through world events each day, deciding which stories to tell, and how, and then tell those stories to millions of people. I began to love having a front row seat to history and the important events unfolding each day. Our ratings, however, were just okay. Because David Westin was trying to figure out what should now happen with the show, I had no promotion or advertising, ever. Unquestionably, the explosion that nearly killed Bob also knocked the two-young-anchors experiment off the rails. I was so consumed, however, with doing the job well *and* being pregnant that I didn't keep my ear to the ground to sense trouble.

At this crucial turn in my career, I still had the same tin ear for office politics that has always been one of my most self-defeating weaknesses. The news division was in flux. Trying to tinker with the formula in an attempt to improve ratings, David Westin told me, "Maybe I'll move Diane [Sawyer] to the evening news anchor and move you to *GMA*. Or maybe I will move Charlie into Bob's seat and the two of you will co-anchor together." There were many such meetings, but I was focused on doing my job each day, not on the bigger picture and all the possibilities that might happen.

Then, on Tuesday, May 23, 2006, I got an email from David Westin during the newscast, asking me to come see him after the show was done.

At seven fifteen I walked into David's office, where he dropped the bombshell: "As of this Friday, you will no longer be anchoring the evening news. I'm going to name Charlie Gibson as anchor. We are going to make an announcement tomorrow. If you wish to leave the network, you can."

I sat in front of him, dumbfounded. Leave the network? I was nearly seven months pregnant. Where was I going to go? What was I going to do? They didn't want me any longer? For a few moments, I couldn't even speak.

"David," I finally said, shaking. "I didn't even want this job. You convinced me to take this. Now you are dumping me?"

I was so upset I can't even remember what he said. I just knew I had to get out of that office, because I did not want to cry in front of him, and the baby was pressing up against my diaphragm, making it hard for me to breathe. In shock, I left his office, went downstairs, numbly collected my things, and got into a cab to go home. I held it together until I walked in the front door of the apartment and then burst into tears, telling Marc what had just happened, hiccupping my way through the entire story. I had been blindsided again, just as in 1997, when I was passed over for *GMA*. To this day I don't know for sure what happened—who lobbied for the anchor chair, how the decision was made.

The behind-the-scenes maneuvering was the cover story in *New York Magazine* and the *Observer*. A book by Howard Kurtz on the evening news wars reported that Charlie had refused to co-anchor with me, and without him to fill in while I was on maternity leave the network was in a very bad place. Charlie had already been passed over for the job once. I think he felt that this time, he deserved the job on his own, and God knows, he had earned it. All I know is that in this high-stakes game of anchor musical chairs, when the music stopped, I was the one left standing without a seat. On that Tuesday night in May, with the public announcement just hours away, I had to act fast. I called my agent, who was equally shocked (not a good sign), and decided with ABC management that I would say the decision to step down was mine, that the duties involved with anchoring the evening news were too much for me, with a three-year-old and a newborn on the way. This way, I could keep my job as co-host of *20/20* when I returned from maternity leave. I felt I had no other option.

I know many people saw through this, but it was the hand I was dealt, and I played it. For the sake of my family, I had to. We needed my salary, not just for the next few months when our baby would be born, but for the next several years. I must also be honest and say that for me at least, the story had the added benefit of being true. I was already struggling with the guilt and the pressure of working long hours with a three-year-old at home. I was deluding myself to think it would not get even more excruciating with a newborn. How would I travel the world covering breaking news with a baby in tow? How would I nurse him and bond with him while staying at the office until ten p.m. three nights a week? There are women today at the cable networks with very young children who anchor nightly shows—Megyn Kelly on Fox and Erin Burnett at CNN, to name two. They make it work somehow, and more power to them! But I didn't feel I could. I didn't feel I had the support at home, and I clearly didn't have the confidence of the news division. With Charlie at the helm of *World News Tonight*, the requirement to stay late to update for the West Coast—was dropped. Neither was he expected to anchor on a regular basis from the field. The decision was made to return to a traditional broadcast—a single anchor, doing a solid show. And it worked. Under Charlie, the news division finally settled after a year of tragedy and turmoil. Ratings ticked up, the tension in the hallways calmed down. I packed up my office and all my dreams for what might have been at *World News Tonight*, moved back to *20/20*, and prepared to give birth to my new son. I had no way of knowing then that this experience had been a relative cakewalk. My most difficult days, and the darkest, were still ahead of me.

—⚏—

PART III

Falling

August 16, 2006, was a warm, sunny day. It was the day I was scheduled to give birth. I had hoped to deliver naturally, but as in the first pregnancy, I showed no signs of impending labor, so a c-section was scheduled on my due date. This time, I knew what to expect. I had carefully packed everything I needed for my four-day stay in the hospital, and the dreaded surgery was at least not a surprise. I also knew what to expect with the recovery. My mother had flown out to be with us, and she, Marc, and I arrived early in the morning at the hospital. There was an emergency delivery of twins in the operating room, so we waited for hours. Marc did the *New York Times* crossword puzzle, and my mom talked about the latest article she had written for her hometown newsletter—while I lay there hooked up to an IV, my anxiety ratcheting up as the hours crawled by. I had too much time to think about the surgery, too much time to worry that something might go wrong. It was my doctor who soothed me that day. As I walked into the operating room trailing my IV pole, knees shaking, she took one look at my face and gave me a long hug, holding me as I sat on the table and the anesthesiologist inserted a thin needle into my spine for the epidural. "It's all going to be okay," she whispered in my ear. "Let's meet your baby."

And just twenty minutes later, we did. He was big and beautiful and blond—I could not believe it! I held him and marveled over our good fortune in the genetic lottery while they stitched me up. He was absolutely perfect. He had huge hands and feet, rosy chubby cheeks, and a perfect cupid's bow for a mouth. We named him Samuel Wyatt Cohn. I kept hospital visitors to a minimum and focused on my baby. I had read about how important skin-to-skin contact is for newborns, so every day I would tuck him inside my nightgown, against my chest, his head nestled under my chin. As with Zachary, nursing was easy. I could have fed an army of babies—I was awash in breast milk, and Sam loved to nurse. I remembered from my time with Zachary how quickly those few weeks of paid maternity leave passed, so I tried to savor every moment with Sam once I got home.

But something was different for me. I was weepy and profoundly exhausted, yet unable to sleep. I would wake up in the middle of the night to nurse, and then toss and turn for the three hours until Sam was due to wake up again. I would lie there, staring at the clock, growing more and more anxious as the minutes ticked by. *I need to sleep! Why can't I sleep?* I was desperate to rest, and I could not. I tried all my old tricks—counting by twos, conjugating Spanish verbs, reciting the rosary. Nothing worked.

I had hired a baby nurse to help me out, and I remember one afternoon bursting into tears while she looked at me with concern. "What's wrong, Elizabeth?" she asked. "I don't know. I am just so sad," I sobbed, "and I am just so tired." After that I called my doctor. I worried I might have postpartum depression. She sent me to an expert, who spent hours examining me before saying, "You are not depressed. You are anxious."

I stared at her, surprised. "That's it? Just anxious? I have been anxious my whole life. I am not having panic attacks. I have had insomnia since I was in college, but never like this, never keeping me awake all night. Why is it so bad now?"

The doctor had a lot of theories—but looking back it's pretty obvious. I had just been demoted at my job in a painful and very public way. I was stressed about what it would be like going back to work. Added to that was the responsibility of supporting my family. I wasn't sleeping more than a few hours at a time. I was so exhausted that I felt like I was losing my mind. I could not think clearly, I was overly emotional, everything seemed dire, and dark.

On top of it all, Marc and I were growing further apart. He was making a new record and was gone a lot, and he was sleeping in the den so he would not be awakened when I would get up to nurse Sam. I felt abandoned. I spent most of my days talking to the baby nurse, who was comforting but temporary and, in reality, a total stranger. When I confronted Marc about the growing chasm between us, he admitted that he had felt I was not there for him when he was shot a year earlier and that he had never really forgiven me for it.

He was right in many ways—once it was clear he was physically fine I had turned my attention back to work and the aftermath of Peter Jennings's death. Marc had needed much more from me emotionally during that time, and I did not see that. I had failed him. "I am so sorry," I said. "I had no idea." He accepted my apology, but nothing really changed. He was distracted and indifferent to me, and I was probably the same way to him. I was not talking to him about my worry and my insecurity, and the humiliation of my demotion was just now truly sinking in. Whenever we did talk, we just seemed to argue.

We settled into a routine as the weeks, months, and eventually years went by...sharing family dinners and time with Zachary and Sam, and then after the boys were in bed, Marc would go to the den to watch TV and I would go to our room to read and fall asleep. We led parallel lives, the trajectories unspooling alongside each other, without ever intersecting in any meaningful way. Had I known that this pattern that started during my second maternity leave would continue, I would have fought harder to change it. But I didn't. Instead, we each retreated to our separate corners to nurse our resentments and grow inexorably apart. The fragile happiness we once enjoyed began to crumble. And into the lonely void, I poured a glass of chardonnay.

—⁓—

Drink, and leave the world unseen.

           —JOHN KEATS, *Ode to a Nightingale*

By the time my maternity leave ended and it was time to go back to ABC, I was beginning to slip back into my habit of drinking a glass or two of white wine every night. I had to manage it carefully, since I was still breastfeeding. I would only have a drink after I had nursed Sam and had enough milk pumped so that I had the whole night to sleep. I had been assured by my doctor that any alcohol would dissipate by the morning, when I would nurse again before going to the office, my breast pump and empty bottles in tow.

I was happy to get back to work, even though I felt that same guilt I had with Zachary each day as I left for the office. But once again, I had no choice. There were bills to pay: a mortgage, child care for both children—all these expenses were my responsibility. I was beginning to feel resentful having to carry that financial burden alone. But I couldn't seem to find a way to talk to Marc about it. The topic of money had become a third rail in our marriage—untouchable. Deadly.

I was incredibly lucky to have my job as co-host of *20/20*. I loved it, and I was well paid. Perhaps the tension over money was a symptom of bigger issues in the marriage. I no longer felt safe and taken care of. I felt alone, and frightened of all the responsibility on my shoulders. Like so many working mothers, I took on a heavy load: working all day, running the household, breastfeeding a baby, being present for my three-year-old, and taking care of the finances. And at the end of each day, I felt I had earned my glass of wine as my reward.

Returning to work also meant adjusting to the reality of my new, diminished role at ABC. By now it was clear to me that relinquishing the anchor chair to Charlie was the best thing for me and for the network. But it didn't make it any easier as I kept bumping into constant reminders that my status had changed. When I asked to interview the president, I was told the network would no longer put my name forward. "Charlie will be doing that," they said, or, "That one is going to Diane." My brief tenure near the top of the list for the big interviews was over. I wasn't even on any list any longer. I had lost my front row seat to history, and I missed it terribly. I tried to focus on doing the best work I could, but now that the shock of my demotion had worn off and the excitement of giving birth had mellowed, the sting of what had happened took over.

I personalized it. I forgot that nearly everyone in television news has had a ride on the wheel—up and then down, and then perhaps up again. I felt like a failure, and it was my fault. I wasn't good enough. I wasn't tough enough. I didn't work hard enough. It was unfair. The thoughts played over and over in my insecure, anxious psyche.

I didn't tell anyone how inadequate I felt—how much like a loser I believed I was. I kept it hidden inside. The only thing that could hold back the bad feelings for a while was alcohol. For a few hours each night, things would be all right. The anxiety and resentment would soften and recede just enough to make it bearable. But the cocoon of a white wine buzz can only take you so far. I was isolated in it, and outside it, my untended problems festered and grew. Alcohol robbed me of the ability to see others— like Marc—and understand what they might be feeling or going through. Drinking to escape was profoundly selfish, and all those unresolved resentments and worries metastasized while I drank to ignore them. My lifelong habit of running from whatever made me anxious or hurt was beginning to backfire. Because now I was running to the refrigerator to pour that glass of wine—sighing with satisfaction as I took that first sip. It was a pattern of escape that would continue for the next three years.

For the most part drinking quieted my emotions;

drinking didn't make me loud or angry, except for a few occasions, like the Nanny Crisis of 2009...

It was nine p.m. Sunday night in late November, Thanksgiving week. The boys were in bed, and Marc was on the road. I was getting everything ready for work the next day, packing my research into my big bag, setting out the cereal bowls for breakfast, and oh yes, sipping my third massive glass of chardonnay. By this time, I was counting my glasses because Marc had begun to notice and protest again that I was drinking too much. So each glass I poured was really more like one and a half—filled to the brim. I had nearly drained the glass when I checked my email and noticed a message from the new nanny, who was supposed to start work the next day. "I have changed my mind about working for your family," it read. "I think I would like to work as a governess instead of as a nanny, so I will not be there tomorrow morning. Thank you anyway for the offer."

I nearly dropped my wineglass. In just a few hours I had to go to work. The sitter sleeping over that night needed to leave in the morning, and I had no one to watch my children. I had no plan B, no family to call— they all lived on the west coast—and no one I knew who could help me out. I know this was a luxury problem—I was lucky to be able to afford a nanny to help me juggle a demanding career with two young children. But this everyday crisis nearly every working mother has had to face completely threw me. All my carefully laid plans were out the window and my husband was out of town. I started to panic, and started to get really, really angry at how out of control my domestic three-ring circus felt. I reached for the phone and called the agency that I had paid a handsome sum to screen and vet this "governess." I let loose with my wine-fueled fury. "Are you fucking kidding me?? What kind of agency is this? This woman is canceling on me less than twelve hours before she is supposed to arrive—this is unacceptable!!" I screamed into the phone. "Fix this now!"

I was beyond reasoning. Underneath, I was anxious, stressed, and overwhelmed—what was I going to do? But my three jumbo servings of wine made it impossible for me to handle this maturely or thoughtfully. All I could do was yell at the poor, apologetic woman on the other line. Zachary heard me and twice got out of bed to walk into the kitchen. He was frightened. "Mommy, is everything okay?" I am ashamed to admit that I didn't comfort him or hug him. I just turned and told him to go back to bed so I could continue my rant on the phone.

That night was my first binge. I waited for several hours for the woman from the agency to make calls and find someone who could show up the next morning to work. As I waited, I drank more. Seething, sipping, fuming, pouring. By the time I got a call around midnight telling me that a nanny named Beverly would arrive the next morning at seven a.m. to work, I had consumed six large glasses of wine. I went to bed drunk that night (thank God my children were not home alone with me) and woke up so hungover I could barely show our new nanny around.

For the first time, running to the gym and sweating out the alcohol was not an option. There was no way I could make it. I tried drinking Gatorade, but I was too nauseated. My head was pounding, and I had the shakes. I had never felt this bad before. I could barely function at work. When I finally got home Monday night, I walked straight to the refrigerator and, with trembling hands, poured myself a glass of wine. It finally steadied my hands and stopped my pounding heart. *This must be what they mean when they say "hair of the dog,"* I thought. Something shifted for me that night, in a dreadful way. I lost my footing and skidded on my backside down a dangerous slope, down into a ditch where drinking more was the only solution I could find to easing my hangover. It would take me years to claw my way back out.

When Marc came home the following day, in the morning, I was still in bed, and he could see that I was very sick from all the alcohol. I went to my doctor, who promptly admitted me into the hospital. I spent a day and two nights that Thanksgiving week in a private room, under a pseudonym, getting IV rehydration and Ativan. Once the wine wore off, I was shocked and horrified at what I had done. When the nurse came in to check my vital signs, I could barely make eye contact. Marc came to visit with the boys, who knew only that Mommy was sick.

When Zachary walked in he had tears in his eyes—he was scared for me. I felt so profoundly guilty as I hugged him and reassured them both that I would be home tomorrow.

I had failed at the most sacred task assigned me—being a good mother. You would have thought that enormous guilt and shame would have led me to swear off alcohol forever. You would be wrong.

I went on to spend the next two years on a campaign of mostly controlled drinking, sprinkled with bouts of sobriety and a handful of terrifying binges. The biggest problem was that I still did not believe I was an alcoholic. I was deeply steeped in denial. *I have a drinking problem*, I thought. *I sometimes drink too much. But I am not an alcoholic.* It's so crazy that as I write it, I can't believe I thought that. But I did, and that kept me from ever seeking help or advice from the very people who knew best how to deal with it: other alcoholics.

Instead, I lived with my secret. I kept doing my job—usually to everyone's satisfaction. I was leading a double life: one as a network news anchor, traveling the world, reporting stories, in front of an intense and unforgiving television camera lens; the other as a woman who was sneaking drinks and hiding it from her husband and her friends. I would be able to string together a few days, sometimes a few weeks, without drinking, and then one night, the thought would pop into my head that it sure would be nice to have a glass of wine before going home from the office. Next thing you know, I was off to the races—perched on a tall stool in an elegant bar, ordering a drink. But try as I might to recapture the amber glow of sipping chardonnay, secret drinking wasn't quite as nice. What used to be luxurious now felt faintly pathetic. I worried that people would notice me sitting and imbibing alone, so I would pretend to be waiting for someone, even feigning a phone call from my phantom friend. "Oh that's all right," I would say gaily into the dead cell phone pressed to my ear. "I just sat down. Take your time. I will meet you there!" I would also take great care to vary the places I went, fearful I would see someone I knew or that the bartender would notice I had been there a few too many times and tip off the gossip columns. WHAT NET-WORK NEWS ANCHOR DRINKS ALONE EVERY NIGHT BEFORE HEADING HOME TO HER FAMILY? The possible headlines made me shudder. But what is astonishing is that the fear of being exposed didn't make me stop. It reminds me of something I read in the book of Alcoholics Anonymous: "However intelligent we may have been in other respects, where alcohol has been involved we have been strangely insane." Instead, I would usually order a second glass, check to make sure I had some breath mints, and then head home . . . my self-imposed isolation growing, along with my lies. My sister tells me it was around this time that I began to disappear from their lives. My secret life—my drinking, my anxiety, my unhappiness, my insecurity—wrapped me up tight. I was caught in a straitjacket of my own making. I did not tell anyone what I was feeling. I did not tell anyone that I was drinking too much to escape those feelings. I didn't call my parents and seek their comfort. I didn't visit my brother or sister to confide in them or ask for their help. I just kept drinking and let everything, and everyone, slip away.

It wasn't until the summer of 2011 that my sister realized there was a problem. She came to visit us in New York, where we were renting a house for a few weeks near the beach. When she arrived with her children after their long trip from Seattle, she knew immediately something was wrong. I was sleepy, and seemed out of it. She was baffled and hurt. She tells me I was a shell of a person, so deep in my own misery I was oblivious to her and everything that was going on in her life—her recent, painful divorce, her struggle to adjust to her new reality, even the eight-hour trip she had just taken with three young children. I took Aimie upstairs and cried and told her how unhappy I was in my marriage, and that I was worried I was drinking too much. Then, exhausted by my confession and the wine I had been drinking steadily that afternoon and evening, I went to sleep. Aimie was shaken. She went downstairs and confronted Marc.

"How long has this been going on?" she demanded. "How long has she been drinking like this?" When Marc told her it had been happening now for a few years, Aimie was distraught.

"Why didn't you tell me? Why didn't you say anything to us?"

Aimie says Marc replied, "I didn't think it was my story to tell." I don't know why Marc never reached out to my family. He was certainly telling his own family and friends about my drinking. Perhaps he just didn't know how to help me and never thought to enlist their support. It is easy to look back with critical eyes. It's not so easy to be in the middle of it all, as he was, wondering how on earth to make it better. Either way, I was not yet willing to admit I needed help, at least not out loud, and you cannot force someone to get help if they are not willing to get it.

Aimie called my mom and dad, and my brother Chris to tell them what was happening. Chris and my parents began to reach out. But I still didn't want to hear their suggestions or seek treatment. Once I sobered up on that trip with Aimie, I didn't want to talk anymore about my unhappiness or my drinking. The small opening I had allowed that first night was now closed. I didn't want to share anymore, and I did not want anyone lecturing me about drinking.

Looking back, it is clear that somewhere along the line, some switch had been flipped. While I had been able early in my marriage to control and cut back my drinking, now it was a struggle. Once I started, I didn't want to stop. I looked upon Marc—and his well-founded criticism of how I drank—as my enemy, someone to be thwarted, certainly not someone in whom I could confide my worries that something was wrong with me—namely, the realization that I could not seem to find another way to ease my stress and calm my anxiety. I drank to escape my unhappiness in our marriage, the loneliness I was feeling in it. And drinking just made the marriage even worse, driving the wedge between us deeper, making it impossible to fix our growing isolation from each other.

Any attempts at controlled drinking went out the window completely when I traveled overseas for work. Then I would find myself liberated by the anonymity of hotel bars in different countries, and I would once again find myself drinking to excess. There was a trip to India to do a story on gendercide—how some families there are rampantly aborting or abandoning baby girls because having a boy brought money and prestige, and having a girl would cost the family an expensive dowry. I drank the entire trip. It was a tremendously important story, and we worked hard at bringing it alive. We visited a village where there were no young women, only men, wondering who they'd ever find to marry. We confronted an operator of an illegal ultrasound clinic, who had a brisk business telling mothers the gender of their unborn baby, so they could then terminate the pregnancy if it was a girl. I grilled government officials on the halfhearted attempts to enforce the laws against gendercide. And yet, when I watch that report, I don't feel proud. I cringe. I look puffy and pale in several of the interviews. I explained it away—it was a grueling shoot in 100-degree temperatures. We all had jet lag, and everyone had food poisoning (actually, I was the only one who didn't; maybe all the booze killed the bacteria).

I was sure my producer and crew must have known I was drinking every night, but no one said a word. I drank the whole long flight home from Delhi. By the time I landed, the combination of too much wine and too little sleep left me unable even to answer the customs agent's questions. "How long were you in India, ma'am?" I stared at him, mute, wracking my foggy brain. How long had I been gone? The agent looked at me closely, then sighed, stamped my passport, and waved me through. I went home, walked in the door, and went straight to bed to sleep off the trip. No hello hugs for the boys, who were eating dinner in the kitchen; no exciting stories of my trip far away. Just another hangover to sleep off, another important moment with my family that I missed. There are so, so many of those moments, and I will never, ever get them back.

If there is any doubt in your mind that alcoholism is a disease, know this: I would die for my children. I love them more than anything in the world. Yet I could not stop drinking for them. I could not stop as the look on my husband's face morphed from dismay to disgust as he saw what I was doing. I could not stop to fix my marriage. I could not stop to save my life. I would not accept that I needed to do something dramatic to change this devastating trajectory. Not until spring break 2012.

That year we took the boys to West Palm Beach,

Florida. Warm weather, soft air, gentle waves, family—
what could be nicer? I arranged five glorious days of sun
and sea. We boarded the plane, and I stowed the tennis
rackets and the Frisbees in the overhead compartment and
settled in for a few rounds of the card game Rat-a-Tat Cat
with Sam, who was sitting next to me.

Suddenly, a thought occurred: *I have worked hard to
pay for this vacation. Wouldn't it be nice to have an afternoon
cocktail on the way there?* And so it came to be that the
orange juice I was sipping was spiked with vodka by the
accommodating flight attendant, up in the galley, where
no one could see. By the time we landed and checked into
the hotel, I was no longer planning games on the beach;
I was plotting how to get another drink. In the process, I
ended up actually drinking more than I intended—gulping
down mimosas while Marc played tennis, swigging a glass
of wine before he and the boys returned from a quick
swim. I even resorted to drinking a beer, which I detest,
because it was the only alcohol left in the mini bar. (By
day 3 I had consumed every alcoholic beverage in there.)

My fantasy family week descended into a hellish few
days at the end where instead of feeling close to my children and husband, I felt—in whatever passed for more
lucid moments—terribly sad and apart, lying all by myself
in bed in a darkened room, drinking, drinking, drinking.

Sam would bound in from the beach, smelling of
sand and sunscreen, heat radiating off his little body.
"Mommy, Mommy!" he would say, standing next to my

pillow. "When are you going to get out of bed?" Not even my intense love for him and Zachary could save me from the consequences of all I had consumed. I was exhausted. When I drink, I get sleepy...so sleepy I simply cannot stay awake. Most people would call it passing out, but it wasn't like I dropped to the floor. I would say "I need to go to bed now," and then nothing—nothing—could get me up until I had slept it off.

Marc was furious, and he had every right to be. Thank God he was a wonderful father to the boys—he spent hours with them at the pool and on the beach, distracting them for a little while from wondering why I wasn't with them. And he had his hands full taking care of me. I wasn't eating, and once again, I was sick from all that alcohol. He arranged through the hotel concierge for a nurse to come see me and make sure I was hydrated. By the time the vacation I had longed for—and then ruined— was over, I could no longer deny that I had a big problem. I was beginning to grow afraid, deep down inside, that I really was powerless over alcohol, that I was losing myself and everyone I loved to it.

When I got home, I summoned up all my courage, called my friend Dana, and told her I needed help. She works in the music business and has known plenty of people who had struggled with addiction. Most importantly, she was the only person in my life at that point who passed no judgment on my appalling behavior. "I love you," she said. "I know a great place for you to go. I will make a call. No matter what you decide to do, I am here for you."

Within days, Dana called back and told me about a treatment center in Utah called Cirque Lodge. She said it was very discreet and highly recommended, and it had an opening for a twenty-eight-day stay. "Wait a minute," I said. "Twenty-eight days? I can't get that kind of time off from work." This is how crazy I was, how deep my denial ran. I was finally willing to get help, but I didn't want to tell anyone what I was doing. I somehow convinced Cirque that I could only come for two weeks, because I could not tell ABC News where I was going. In my mind I had an alcohol problem. I wasn't an *alcoholic*, so I didn't need the full program. I was dipping my toe into recovery, when I should have been jumping in like my hair was on fire (and figuratively, it was). I told my bosses I needed some surgery—nothing life threatening, but definitely requiring a couple weeks off. I told no one where I was going—only Marc, Dana, and my parents, brother, and sister knew. At the end of April, just weeks after our disastrous trip to Florida, I packed my bags and headed to Utah for my secret stab at sustaining sobriety.

—☳—

Denial ain't just a river in Egypt.

—ATTRIBUTED TO MARK TWAIN

Cirque Lodge sits in the shadow of Mount Timpanogos in the picture-postcard setting of Sundance, Utah. It's the same village where Robert Redford holds his annual film festival. Movie stars, moguls, and other celebrities gather there each year for glittering parties and must-see premieres. Just down the road is a small lodge where people gather for something else: recovery and freedom from addiction. I arrived terrified, my heart pounding in my ears, so ashamed that I had a hard time answering simple questions, like "Why are you here?" "Because I drink too much," I mumbled. I stood, watching a staff member search my luggage, in case I had tried to stash a bottle of wine underneath my jeans and sweatshirts. All medication of any kind was confiscated. Even aspirin and multivitamins would be dispensed by the staff. I wandered into the main living room and awkwardly stood to the side, trying not to look at the handful of people sitting around. I felt so embarrassed to be there; I assumed everyone else must feel the same way.

"Hi! You must be new!" I turned and saw a pretty woman with long brown hair. "I'm Anne. Here, I will show you around." Anne took me from room to room, introducing me to people on the way, pointing out the coffeepot, the library, the meeting rooms, and an airy top-floor perch with 360-degree views of the mountains. It was beautiful. She led me outside to the yard, where there was a gazebo, and in it, a small group was sitting around smoking. "This is the butt hut," she said, gesturing. "It's the only place you are allowed to smoke." A couple of the smokers turned to look our way, slowly exhaling. "Um, I don't smoke," I said apologetically.

Memories of grade school cliques and being the odd girl out came flooding in, like they were yesterday. Anne laughed. "That's okay! The yard goes around the other side. There is a fountain there that's really nice." At that point, a man appeared on the deck. "Meeting starts in ten minutes," he called out. "Bring your notebooks."

Things moved fast at Cirque. There were twelve other alcoholics at the lodge, and it was the first time in my life that I was surrounded—day in and day out—by people who were struggling exactly like I was, who had horror stories exactly like mine. I was able to finally talk about what I had done—the vacations I had ruined, the trips to the hospital, the flights I could barely remember—and not feel like the confession was going to kill me.

Most of the people in our group at Cirque were, like

me, what are called highly functional addicts. They had managed to hold demanding jobs, running companies or achieving fame in the sports or entertainment industries, all while keeping their addiction a secret. I might have just dipped my toe in at Cirque that spring, but I did learn something very, very valuable: that I was not the only one with this terrible secret. I was not terminally unique, as I remember hearing someone call it. It was an enormous relief, because it helped defuse the shame just a tiny bit.

I had a wonderful therapist assigned to me. Her name was Ingrid. She was the first person I met with whom I felt I could be completely honest. I told her about my lifelong anxiety and insecurity. I confessed I was unhappy in my marriage and didn't know what to do. I told her I drank because I was in so much pain I would do anything not to feel it. And she was just as honest with me.

"I think you are making a mistake not staying here the full four weeks," she said one day, as we were wrapping up our session.

I was startled. "What? You know I can't stay longer. My boss doesn't know I am here."

"Not telling him was a mistake," she said firmly. "You can't treat alcoholism in two weeks. Most people need two months, or more."

At that point she might as well have been speaking Greek. There was no way I was staying two months, or even one. And despite my ten days thus far at Cirque, I still wasn't even convinced I was a true alcoholic.

I remember sitting in a lecture on alcohol and the brain with Will, a man who was also there to stop drinking. He was one of my favorite people at Cirque, a successful businessman with a gentle way and an easy smile, who loved mountain biking as much as I did. The lecturer was pointing to a chart that had horizontal lines on it, bisected in the middle, with symptoms listed on either side. On the left side were alcohol abusers; on the right, alcoholics. Will and I sat there, debating among ourselves. "Which side are you on?" I whispered. "The problem drinker, or the alcoholic?"

"I think I am on the problem drinker side," he said. "But right up next to the line that delineates an alcoholic."

"Me too," I answered back.

Even in rehab, even among other alcoholics, even with the memory of my recent binge still fresh, I clung to the idea that I wasn't really an alcoholic and that maybe someday I could still drink normally, like everyone else.

The two weeks at Cirque flew by. In many ways, it was a wonderful experience. Each day we split into groups to talk about how we had lost control of our drinking and our lives. We filled notebooks with writing assignments in which we shared our deepest, darkest secrets. We wrote out timelines, tracing our relationship with alcohol, and examples of how it derailed us. At one point, we were instructed to write a farewell letter to whatever substance we had abused. At first we laughed. "You're kidding, right? A letter?" But soon we got to work. This is what I wrote.

Dear Chardonnay,

You have been in my life for many years. You were my comfort and my friend. When I was anxious, you soothed me. When I was stressed, you relaxed me. When I was happy, you celebrated with me. When I was angry, you fanned the flames of my fury. You made me feel confident, you gave me courage when I was shy or insecure. You were at the table with me and my girlfriends when we were laughing and having fun. You were by my side at restaurants during romantic dinners with my husband. But something has shifted. I need more of you now to get those feelings from you, and you have begun to exact a creeping, painful toll for your rewards. I don't feel as good now when you are by my side, and I feel truly awful after you have left. When you are gone, I don't like what I see in the mirror: my outer, physical self, and my inner self. You make me feel guilty. You have embarrassed me. You have made me forget things, slur my words, act silly and selfish. But most of all, you have distracted me from my two precious boys and have made me ashamed of myself. It is time we part ways. Please don't try to tempt me with your alluring promises that just a little won't hurt...because you really are not welcome any longer. Move on to those who just want a little of you, and leave me and my family alone.

Firmly, Elizabeth

As we all took turns reading our letters aloud to the group, I was struck by how similar they were...whether they were addressed to alcohol, or cocaine, or heroin. Whether the author was a movie star or an NBA player or a CEO. We had all been brought to our knees by our inability to say no to something that was killing us.

Needless to say, we bonded—drinking tea and munching M&M's from a giant bowl at night, and laughing more than I ever dreamed possible. We were outside in the gorgeous mountains every day—hiking, biking, horseback riding.

Being outdoors in such beauty, I began for the first time in years to feel closer to God, and I listened carefully as the therapists at Cirque spoke of how recovery often meant reconnecting with God or nature—something bigger than us, bigger than the issues we were drinking to avoid. But all too soon, it was time for me to go home. Back to New York, back to the real world, back to all my old problems and fears and anxieties.

As it turned out, I did not stay long enough. I had not fully accepted that I needed to change the way I ran from my pain and numbed it...no exceptions. I did not continue meeting with other alcoholics to hear their wisdom about how to navigate the world without the crutch of a glass of wine. I blithely waved goodbye and walked right back into my secret life. Within two months, I was drinking again.

—◊◊—

Blackout

There are some drinkers for whom blacking out is not unusual. Sarah Hepola writes in her book, aptly named *Blackout*, that she did so the very first time she drank. She describes it as a trapdoor, "a curtain, falling in the middle of the act, leaving minutes, and sometimes hours in the dark." In all my years of drinking I had never had that exact experience.

I always had at least a vague idea of what I did and said the night before. I was usually able to fit things into a reasonably complete narrative, with a patchwork quilt of clues: there was an email I had sent ("God, why did I say that?"), where exactly I had left my clothes (neatly put away meant a pretty good night, dumped in a corner of the bathroom, not so much). Slowly the sodden manuscript of the evening before would float to the surface for me to see.

But, on July 7, 2012, I lost an entire afternoon and night of my life. Gone. Erased. Thirteen hours wiped out, like they had never happened...except they did.

It was Friday, a gorgeous summer day. I had a *20/20* shoot scheduled for late morning, and I woke up feeling drained and miserable. My head was pounding and my mouth felt like it was full of cotton. Things weren't good at home. Marc knew I was drinking again, and he was angry, disgusted, and at his wits' end. We were not even speaking, and instead of acting like an adult and confronting the tension and unhappiness head-on, I had spent the night before drinking to escape. Now, as I poured a cup of coffee and read over my research, I was paying the piper.

A car was downstairs waiting to take me to the shoot. I got in, buckled my seat belt, and took a deep breath. I still felt absolutely miserable. Dully I wracked my brain. *What can I do to make myself feel better?* The traffic slowed at one point, and I spotted a wine store, right next to a pharmacy, and like a thunderbolt, a sly thought occurred to me.

"Can you pull over for a minute please?" I asked. "I need to run into the pharmacy. I'll just be a moment."

But I didn't dash into the drugstore for Advil. Instead, I ducked into 67 Wine and Spirits and bought a bottle of chardonnay and stashed it inside my purse.

I spent the rest of the ride to the set studying my notes for the shoot. It was a straightforward interview, and I had already done my homework. But in the back of my mind I was thinking about that bottle, nestled between my billfold and my reading glasses.

The shoot took a couple of hours. While the crew wrapped, I went into a room off to one side. No one else was there. I pulled out the wine, opened it, and filled a water glass nearly to the brim. I could barely wait for the relief from physical and emotional misery that it would bring. And it delivered. I remember sitting in that room, listening to the crew breaking down just outside the door, and drinking the chardonnay. It felt like I was sliding into a place where I could forget that my heart was breaking. I was oblivious to how wrong it was to escape like this, how destructive. Instead I poured myself a second glass. The last thing I remember from that day is tucking the bottle back into my purse, saying goodbye to the crew, and getting into a waiting car, and putting my seat belt on... and that's where the screen goes blank.

At three the next morning, I woke up. I was in a small room with just a sink and a metal gurney. I was lying on top of it in a blue hospital gown, covered with a flimsy blanket. I sat up, wide awake, wary, completely baffled about where I was or how I got there. There was an orderly sitting outside. I crept to the door, clutching the gown shut around my body.

"Where am I? What time is it?"

"You are at St. Luke's hospital emergency room."

I was desperate to be in my apartment, in my own bed, anywhere but here. "Where are my clothes? I need to go home."

The orderly returned with my orange sweater and my white skirt, still spotless, folded neatly. He also brought my high heels. I put everything on, feeling bizarrely over-dressed, and still with no clue as to what happened.

"Do you have my purse?" I asked.

"No, this is all you came in with," he answered, motioning to the clothes I was now wearing. I looked around desperately. I had no phone, no money, no way to get home, no way to call for help.

"Please, can I borrow your phone?" I asked. I dialed home. Marc answered after a few rings, sounding exhausted and resigned. He told me to stay where I was until morning, that he would not come in the middle of the night to get me. After hanging up, I briefly considered walking home, alone. Fifty blocks in high heels, in the middle of the night. Instead, I lay back down and waited. I spent the next four hours alone in that grim room with my increasingly anxious thoughts.

Why can't I remember anything?

I was too embarrassed to ask the orderly what happened, and there was something in his face when he said the doctor wanted to see me before I left. There was also something in the sound of my husband's defeated voice on the phone.

Over the next two days, I learned what happened or, at least, parts of it. Like a steel door, the rest of it locked shut on me. I have spent months trying to coax or pry a memory from around the edges of that door, and I cannot. Here is what I have been told happened: late afternoon

Friday, a woman driving down Riverside Drive spots me someplace along the park. She pulls over and offers me a ride home. I am able to tell her where I live. By the time she arrives at my apartment building, I am unconscious. A superintendent carries me into the lobby while the frantic doorman calls Marc. The woman tells Marc she picked me up because she saw two sketchy-looking men hanging around me nearby. Marc waits for an ambulance with me, watching me breathe, terrified that at any moment my breath will cease. Our nanny keeps my two children upstairs, far away from the scene unfolding in the lobby; their mother is drunk, passed out for everyone to see, in the lobby of her own building. Once at the emergency room, tests show I have a blood alcohol level that is usually lethal: 0.4.

I still have no idea how much wine I drank that day. Nor do I have any idea where I went when I finished the shoot, nor what I did. All I do know is how lucky I am for what didn't happen that day: I wasn't robbed or raped in the park while unable to defend myself, and because that woman brought me home, I didn't die from alcohol poisoning. For the first time, I was truly terrified. I needed help.

Clearly, the people at Cirque were right when they had said two weeks was definitely not enough; I needed to go back for the full twenty-eight days. I knew there was no putting off telling ABC where I was going and why. I could no longer keep my addiction a secret. I called my agent and told him everything. I spoke to Barbara Fedida, the ABC News executive in charge of talent, on the phone. She was warm and sympathetic. She did not press me for details; she was simply reassuring.

"Take this time to get better. We are here for you when you get back."

Why, oh why had I not trusted in their support on my first secret visit to Cirque?

As I packed my suitcases for Utah once again that Sunday evening, the phone rang a second time. This time it was Ben Sherwood, the new president of the news division. Under his leadership, ABC News was reinvigorated—people were excited to work there, and the ratings on all our programs were on the upswing. Ben is smart, driven, and, that night, direct.

"When you took a couple of weeks off two months ago, was that about this, too?"

It would have been wrong to evade any further.

"Yes. I was trying to keep it a secret."

"What are you addicted to?"

I caught my breath. He was the first person who ever straight out asked me that.

"Well…it's alcohol," I stammered. And then in that moment, flustered, I added, "and Ambien, too." I thought simply being an alcoholic didn't sound very feminine. It just shows how completely crazy I was. Instead of being frightened to my core about the fact that I nearly died, I was worried my boss would think I was a garden-variety drunk. Truth be told, there is nothing feminine about a woman who has had too much to drink. I had been there and seen many others there, too: voices ringing a little too loud, eyeliner slightly smeared, lipstick tattooing the rims of too many glasses on the table, and the perilous trip to the ladies' room—eyeing the floor like it's a sheet of ice, praying you don't sway or stumble in your stilettos.

Ben's voice on the phone interrupted my shame-filled reverie.

"I am going to have to tell Anne Sweeney [the president of the network]. This could affect our plans for when Robin starts her treatment."

Robin Roberts, the co-host of *Good Morning America*, had just revealed she had been diagnosed with myelodysplastic syndrome. It is a rare blood disorder, and she would need a bone marrow transplant to save her life. She would begin an extended medical leave in just six weeks, and would be in the fight of her life for months. Ben had asked me to help fill in on *GMA* while she was gone.

I swallowed hard. "I understand, Ben. Thank you so much for your support."

"You have it, Elizabeth. We are all rooting for you. Take whatever time you need."

So I packed my bags and went back to Utah for the full program. As I drove the winding road up into the mountain for a second time, I was embarrassed to be returning so soon, but also relieved. I knew how lucky I was to get this second chance in this beautiful place to try to find a lasting sobriety.

Right away, Cirque had me meet with one of the towering figures in the world of recovery, Earl Hightower. His story of addiction is so harrowing it leaves you breathless. Yet he tells his tale of descent to the very bottom and his ultimate redemption with such candor, humanity, and humor—yes, humor! He had the room laughing uproariously one moment (*Oh my God, he really did that?*) and so still the next you could hear a pin drop (*Oh my God, he really survived that?*). Earl sat me down one afternoon.

"Elizabeth, do you know how close you came to dying? It's unbelievable you survived. Do you understand that?"

Actually, it was hard for me to understand. I could not remember any of it. It felt like someone else's story. Earl leaned in.

"You cannot have another drink in your life. Ever. You are just like me. We cannot drink safely."

And with that dire admonition, I spent the next twenty-eight days working as hard as I could on my recovery. I worked with the therapists there, trying to detangle my lifelong anxiety, trying to learn how not to let it overrun me, how to find some other way to deal with it, and with my unhappiness, without alcohol. I had my own room and was able to sleep, deeply, every night, and despite the heat outdoors, I was biking or hiking every day. They encouraged exercise there—if you feel healthy and strong physically, it pays off emotionally. All my life working out had been one of the positive ways I relieved stress and anxiety. Being in all that natural beauty—away from television, electronics, newspapers, the daily distractions of a full and busy life—left me time to absorb the natural world and appreciate it. It was spiritual for me, that space...not just around me, but inside me, because life had slowed down. It was my father who pointed out to me on the phone one day that this was the first time in my life that I had gotten off the treadmill on which I always seemed to sprint.

"Think of it, honey," my dad said. "You started working in high school during the summers, and started your first job the day after you graduated from college. You have gone from one job to the next for twenty-eight years without ever taking a break!"

I had never realized that. It was too soon for me to see how that inability to slow down and breathe in life had fed my anxiety and my addiction. That insight would come later. But those four weeks at Cirque gave me my first glimpse that racing through my days, always focused on what was coming up next, meant that I missed a lot of what was happening right around me.

I remember telling Marc about that one night. I was allowed to Skype with Marc and the boys every night for a short time. It was an unusual arrangement for any rehab facility to allow, but I had not told my children where I was—they thought I was on a long shoot—and I missed them desperately. Being able to see and talk to them nearly every day allowed me to relax and focus on the work I was doing. I felt I had Marc's support and even affection during that stay. I told him one night that the essay I had written about being powerless over alcohol had gotten great feedback from the counselors. "Are you getting an A in rehab?" he teased. We both laughed, the joke on me—ever the worker, ever the perfectionist.

Twice a week, Cirque would invite a group of people who were recovering alcoholics over for dinner. They seemed to represent every walk of life—a chic woman in riding boots, a young man who built and raced bicycles, a crusty cowboy who never took off his hat. After dinner we would sit around the living room, the sun setting on the mountains through the floor-to-ceiling windows, and go around the room sharing our stories of addiction. On my last weekend at Cirque, it was my turn to share. To my surprise, my eyes filled with tears—I always hated showing any emotion. It made me feel naked, exposed.

"I am leaving in three days, and I am really scared." The room got very quiet. The faces looking back at me were sympathetic. "I am afraid of going back to my life, of being surrounded by stress and temptation. I am afraid of my anxiety, and what I will do to escape it."

An elderly man, grizzled and gray, was sitting next to

me. He put his calloused hand on my head, like my father did when I was still a little girl.

"God bless you," he said. "Pray to God to help you." In that moment, I had never felt closer to someone than I did to him. I didn't even know his name.

My last day at Cirque started before dawn. One of the administrators there, Dan, had invited me to go on a hike. I agreed, thinking it would be like every other hike I had done while I was there, but when we got to the base of the mountain at seven a.m., I realized this was very different. We were hiking a mountain—an entire mountain, from the bottom to the very top.

"Are you up to it?' he asked, smiling.

"Of course!" I shot back, brimming with bravado. I laced up a pair of borrowed hiking boots, and we packed food and water into our backpacks and set off. After two hours, the sun had burned off the morning fog and a bit of my confidence. This was hard. I stripped off my fleece and tied it around my waist. On we went, hiking through brambles and wildflowers, up through dense trees, across narrow paths set into steep ravines. We spoke little—the effort to climb took all our strength. After three hours we stopped to eat. I looked up. The summit seemed no closer than when we started.

"How long is this going to take?"

"Last time I hiked it, it was about nine hours to get up and back," Dan answered.

Nine hours?? I wasn't sure I could make it, but I wasn't about to say so. I looked up again at the distant summit.

"Okay then." I got up and took another swig of water and shook out my legs. "Let's go."

For the next four hours we hiked up and up. The trees grew sparse, the path rockier until after a while there was no path at all. At a certain point I stopped looking up at the top; I concentrated on the ground in front of me—on putting one foot in front of the other. My calves were aching, and I felt blisters blooming on my heels where they rubbed against the unfamiliar boots. Dan stopped to rest. He was sweaty and red faced, out of breath in the thin mountain air.

"You keep going," he called out. "I'll catch up."

I had no choice but to keep going. If I stopped to rest now I would never get back up. The muscles aching throughout my body would cramp. So I leaned into the mountain, and on I went. One step at a time, steadily, timed to my own breath. Inhale, step left, exhale, step right. Farther and farther up I climbed, until the air grew chilly and the wind picked up, the sound of it humming through the few pine trees left. Finally, in the afternoon, exhausted and exhilarated, I stumbled over the last ledge and reached the summit. I was alone at the top of the world. There was a pond of water, so clear and still that you could see the fish darting around beneath the clouds reflected on the surface. I sat down at the edge of it and waited for Dan. It was only then, as I leaned against a rock and turned my face up to the sun, that I realized this hike, this test of physical endurance, was a metaphor for recovery: one step at a time, one day at a time. Don't look up at the whole mountain, or your whole life without the crutch of alcohol can seem too much. Just focus on what is right in front of you. Focus on that next step, and do the next right thing.

—៣—

Back in the Swing

Leaving Cirque was bittersweet. I felt safe there, strong and supported. But I knew that I had been living in a bubble for a month—an artificial world that didn't have rough edges and leave bruises. At the airport, as I reached for a bottle of water from the cooler in the deli stand, my hand brushed past a line of small bottles of white wine, chilled and ready. I jerked back for a moment, surprised that I would be confronted so quickly and so innocuously with my drink of choice. I grabbed an Evian, paid the cashier, and allowed myself a moment to feel proud that I wasn't tempted. As I boarded the plane home, I was excited to get back to New York—I couldn't wait to see my family. But my therapist's last words to me echoed, troubling me.

"I think you need to see a therapist who specializes in post-traumatic stress."

I looked at her, startled. "Post-traumatic stress? That's what veterans have, people who have been through terrible life trials. Nothing like that has happened to me."

"Just do yourself a favor and look into it, okay?"

By the time the plane landed in New York, the memory of that conversation had faded. I was beside myself with happiness to be home. I could not stop hugging Zachary and Sam, every time they walked past me. Marc was warm, and welcoming. We all went out to the beach on Long Island for a few days. It was August—the hazy, humid last weeks of summer when it seems half of New York City has left town, fleeing the heat. The family photos from our trip to the beach that year are among my favorites. We look happy, healthy, sun-kissed, lucky. But after just three days at home I got a phone call from the chief publicist for ABC News, Jeffrey Schneider.

"Hey there," he said. "I hate to do this, but we got a call from Cindy Adams. She got a tip from someone that you were away getting help for some sort of issue. She is going to go with a story, and wants a comment. I think you should issue a statement, saying, 'Like millions of Americans, I have struggled with alcoholism,' and say you went to rehab."

I was stunned. I am not naïve about the fact that people in TV news do call columnists and gossip pages to plant rumors and stories. It had happened to me before when I was at *GMA*. But this wasn't another nasty story about me as a journalist; it was a personal story about a deeply painful issue for me and my family. It was no one's business where I had been or what my family and I were going through. I dug in.

"Jeffrey, my own children don't know I was in rehab. I am not going to announce to the world where I was or why. I do not have to share my deepest secrets. My children deserve privacy, and so do I."

Jeffrey is brilliant at his job, and he argued strongly that I should just issue the statement and put it all behind me. But I prevailed. Cindy Adams, who has a column that is syndicated nationwide, did write a story, saying, "People are wondering where has Elizabeth Vargas been these past four weeks," and "whispers in the hallways at ABC" about some sort of health issue. But that's as far as she went. I felt I had won the battle that time. I would go on to later lose the war.

By mid-August, I was back at work at ABC, doing a job I continued to love and felt fortunate to have. Mercifully, no one asked me where I had been, although I am sure most of them had heard those "whispers." We all just got right back to business, telling amazing stories on *20/20*. Starting September 1, I also began filling in for Robin Roberts as co-host of *Good Morning America*. Robin had begun her medical leave, preparing for her bone marrow transplant. No one was sure how long she would be out, literally fighting for her life. Amy Robach and I were asked to rotate weeks hosting the show for the foreseeable future.

As I had been when Peter was on leave, battling cancer, I was honored to fill in...happy to take on two jobs at once. And I loved working with the cast and crew of *GMA*, just as much as with my own crew at *20/20*. The *GMA* hours are grueling—but there is something strangely intimate about everyone rolling into the studio in the pre-dawn, bleary, dressed in jeans and sweatshirts…and the hustle and bustle as you get ready for the high-wire act of two hours of live television.

It was an exciting time to be co-hosting on the show. Robin, George Stephanopoulos, Sam Champion, Josh Elliott, and Lara Spencer had managed to surpass the *Today* show in ratings several times already that year. During the fall of 2012, that lead solidified and became permanent. In November, *GMA* won its first sweeps period in eighteen years. It was amazing and gratifying to be part of it.

All during that fall, I was busy, and happy, and so it was easy for me to stay sober. I had learned (finally!) that I should not drink, and with everything going so well at work and even at home, there was no raging anxiety, no misery to send me running for relief.

But that season of good luck and goodwill could not possibly last. Life doesn't work that way. I was not, as had been recommended, going to meetings with other alcoholics to buttress my sobriety and strengthen my recovery. I had for a while—right when I got home from Cirque—furtively entering and slouching in the back, rarely raising my hand to join the discussion. I was anxious to preserve my anonymity, especially at a time when I was now hosting a national broadcast for two hours every morning. After a few months, I stopped going. I took my eye off the ball. While I was enjoying my new, sober, exciting life, I was doing nothing to ensure I could stay sober once fortune threw a curveball in my direction.

—◦—

Outfoxed

I don't remember what my resolution was on New Year's Eve at the end of 2012. I would like to think that I pledged to do everything I could to guard my sobriety. I might have. But if I did, I joined millions of others who vowed to get in shape, or lose weight, or spend more time smelling the roses, and then failed.

I do remember that in early 2013 my time filling in on *GMA* was nearing an end. Robin had defied the odds and beaten cancer yet again with strength that left everyone in awe. As the date of her return in late February approached, my attention was increasingly taken with another huge story I had been covering for ABC News for the past five years: the murder trials in a fifteenth-century Italian courtroom of a young American named Amanda Knox. She was the college student who had been accused of murdering her British roommate, Meredith Kercher, in Perugia, Italy, in November 2007. It was a story that encompassed three countries and set off an international furor. The media on both sides of the Atlantic could not get enough—headlines alleging satanic rituals, sex games, and drugs appeared almost daily in those first months. There were breathless accounts that Knox, salaciously nicknamed "Foxy Knoxy," was a beautiful, privileged, arrogant American, who instead of studying her junior year abroad, decided to party her way through it.

Leaks from the Italian prosecutor in the case fueled torrid stories of murder and sexual mayhem on the night of November 1, All Saints' Day. Foxy Knoxy and her Italian boyfriend, the police alleged, had slashed Kercher's throat when she refused to participate in their drug-fueled sex games. It wasn't just the brutality of the crime or the lurid tales of what happened in the bedroom crime scene, there was also a geopolitical overlay to the story. The Iraq War, led by the United States, had already grown deeply unpopular in Europe. The "coalition of the willing" (another name for our allies) was restive and resentful of our country's policies around the world. In Italy, Americans were often perceived as entitled, even obnoxious. And in late 2007, much of that negative perception was pinned squarely on Knox. The story, set against the backdrop of an ancient Umbrian town, could have been ripped straight from the pages of Shakespeare.

My *20/20* team and I jumped on it.

It immediately became clear as we investigated that there were problems with those early headlines. The prosecutor slowly stopped talking about satanic rituals (he told me years later he had never even said such a thing). Videotapes taken by the police themselves showed the evidence at the crime scene had been grossly mishandled. Knox wasn't a rich American—she had worked several jobs while at school to pay for her year studying abroad. Even her scandalous nickname, "Foxy Knoxy," turned out to be rather innocent. She had earned it years earlier on a sports field as a crafty soccer player. But what struck me, and gave me the most doubt about the case against Amanda Knox, was the utter lack of any of her DNA in the room where the murder took place. There was plenty of DNA from the victim, Meredith Kercher. And there was DNA everywhere from another young Italian man later convicted of the crime. It's simply impossible to selectively clean your own DNA (which you can't even see) and leave everyone else's behind.

We were the first major news outlet to air doubts about the case against Amanda Knox, in an hour-long special. I was the first journalist to interview her shell-shocked parents, who had flown to Perugia to support her and would go on to spend their life savings paying for her defense. I was in the subterranean courtroom for Knox's testimony and for the verdicts of not one but two of her murder trials in Italy. I remember standing up the hill from the courthouse when the first guilty verdict was announced. It was nearly midnight in Italy, close to the start of the six thirty p.m. newscast in New York. I was in front of a live camera, my image beaming via satellite to New York, waiting to do a live special report of the verdict—the story was that big. Nearly all of the reporters from all the countries covering the story thought there would be an acquittal. The evidence against Knox was too compromised. Then my cell phone buzzed. A single word came through on text: Guilty. At that moment, I heard a huge cheer go up. A large, unruly crowd had gathered outside the courthouse—the people there were clapping and shouting "murderer!" It sounded like a lynch mob. Within minutes I was on live television reporting the news, showing video of a weeping Knox being led back to prison, and the crowd yelling and jostling Knox's mother and father as they fought to get to their car. It was surreal. Hours later, at two a.m., I interviewed Knox's father about the verdict. He was distraught, shaking, his eyes filled with tears of anger and frustration as he protested she was innocent.

I interviewed her friends, her sisters, her defense lawyers, and her prosecutors over the five years her case took to wend its way through the Italian judicial system— convictions, appeals, retrials, and eventual acquittal.

Now Amanda Knox, home and free, was coming out with a book about her case and was about to grant her first interview. The competition was beyond intense. It would make news in this country and in Europe—big news. Each network sent a detailed, polished proposal to Knox, her lawyer, and her publisher, arguing their case.

When the president of ABC's booking team showed our proposal to me, I was impressed and hopeful. It read, in part, "No other television anchor has been as committed to this story as Elizabeth Vargas. She has been on

the story since day one, traveling to Perugia seven times
with her same dedicated team of ABC producers, who
all bring a level of knowledge, commitment and understanding to this story that is unmatched. Most important,
over the years the Knox family has come to know and
trust Elizabeth and the entire ABC News team for their
unceasing passion, dedication and integrity on this story."
Oh my gosh, I thought to myself, *I may actually win this
one!* I allowed myself to begin to believe that five years of
working on this story would actually pay off. My producers and I began strategizing about how we would structure
our final hour on Amanda Knox, the last of many, this
one with her participation.

And then one morning in early February, as I hosted
GMA for one of my last few weeks there, the end game
began. At eight fifteen, while still on the air, I received an
email from Eric Avram, the executive in charge of booking all of ABC's most important interviews.

"I need to speak with you after the show," he wrote.

"Sure," I answered. "What about?"

"Better in person," he said.

"No," I wrote back. "Tell me now!" My heart raced.
I knew this could not be good. I had to struggle to stay
focused on anchoring the last minutes of the show.

"I am coming to the studio. Will meet you there," he
replied.

I waited in my dressing room as Eric made his way
from the headquarters on Sixty-sixth Street to our set in

Times Square. I already knew in my bones that he was bringing bad news, that we hadn't gotten the booking. I wracked my brain—how did NBC beat us? Could it be CBS? What could they offer that we could not? Finally, Eric arrived. He closed the door. It was just the two of us. I was right. I had lost the booking, but not to NBC or CBS, but to my ABC colleague Diane Sawyer.

I stared at Eric, dumbfounded.

"I am so sorry, Elizabeth. I know how hard you worked on this story, but they want Diane. We tried to insist it be you, but they said it had to be Diane or they were going to another network."

"Who? Who insisted?" I asked. I could not believe the Knox family would do this.

"It's Amanda's lawyer."

"Can I talk to him? He's never even met me. Can I persuade him? Doesn't he know I know more about this case than anyone?"

Eric's face was deeply sympathetic.

"He won't meet with you," Eric explained, apologetically.

"Call his bluff! Tell him it has to be me, I am the one who has covered this story from the very start!"

Eric shook his head. "We tried everything. It's done. ABC has agreed it will be Diane. We can't lose this interview to another network."

I argued. I raged. And finally, the sting of the rejection burning so deep, I did the one thing I never allowed myself to do at work, the one thing I hate to do. I burst into tears. As word spread throughout ABC, members of my producing team came in to my office that day to commiserate or console. Diane called to say how terrible she felt about the whole thing—she hadn't lobbied for this, not at all. She was warm, and empathic, and tried to comfort me. She too had lost interviews in past booking wars. She knew how it felt. Yet, despite Diane's sympathy, there was no escaping the simple truth: I had been passed over for a bigger star. I had worked as hard as humanly possible, and my work had been stellar. And it still wasn't enough.

News of the scoop hit the press, with several reporters noting it was I who had worked the story. "Years of jostling among television networks for the first on-camera interview of Amanda Knox ended Monday with ABC emerging the victor," wrote the *New York Times*. "Diane Sawyer will conduct the interview...One of Ms. Sawyer's colleagues, Elizabeth Vargas, led the coverage on ABC, which included several prime-time specials."

I had to stop reading. I had to get out of the office.

I walked up Columbus Avenue, and numbly went into Intermix and bought a scarf, then up the block to L'Occitane and got some hand cream. I hoped it would make me feel better. It didn't. I was devastated, plain and simple. On top of it, I was exhausted. I had been up since four a.m. to host GMA. Hungry, angry, lonely, tired. HALT is the acronym. In recovery, they say that feeling any of those four things means you are in the danger zone—vulnerable to succumbing to the temptation of a drink. That February night, at six p.m., as I wandered in the cold on Columbus Avenue with my shopping bags, I was all four of those things. But I didn't go to a meeting with other alcoholics to feel better. I didn't call a friend. I didn't pray to God for resilience and strength. What I did do is walk into a bar and order my first drink in six months.

I only had one glass of wine that night, and I didn't have another for many weeks. But that slip was the start. That weakness, when I allowed a terrible day at work to lead to a terrible decision to drink, led to an eventual crumbling of my resolve. I was not ready for the bad days or the low blows that everyone in life encounters at some point.

It was just a matter of time before I had slipped back into my old ways—stopping on my way home from work for a secret glass of wine. Or two. First it was just a couple nights a week. Months later, it was every night. It was hardly enjoyable, as I think back. Picking out a table hidden in the corner. Peering anxiously around for anyone who might know me. Eyeing my watch, gauging my time, rifling through my purse for Altoids to cover the smell of chardonnay.

I managed to stop drinking a few times, for a couple of weeks here, a whole month there. But I could never make it last, and by the time summer melted into fall I was buying bottles of wine and hiding them under my bathroom sink.

So much for the romance of sipping a golden elixir from a beautiful piece of stemware while a steady amber glow settles over your world. There I was, in the harsh overhead light, standing over the sink, staring in the bathroom mirror at the miserable woman in the glass, gulping down her wine from a plastic cup.

I looked in my own eyes and knew this could not possibly continue.

———

On My Own in a Mess of My Own Making

The white van creeps up the winding backwoods road, its windows opaque with steam, the air inside warm and close. It is early November. I am wedged in the third row between two young women who are belting out the lyrics of a song by the band One Republic, playing so loud on the radio it is distorted. *"I-I-I-I feel something so right, doing the wrong thing..."* they loudly sing in unison, joined by nearly every one of twelve women in the van. *"I couldn't lie, couldn't lie, couldn't lie, everything that kills me makes me feel alive."* My God, what a lyric. I feel faintly carsick. For about the one thousandth time that week, I wonder how the hell I got here.

"Here" is a rehab facility in rural Tennessee, and if I would cut the crap and step outside of my misery for a moment, I would know precisely how I got here from that first slip back in February. I don't exactly remember what happened at the very end, but I know what I have been told... and slivers of my latest horror show of drinking poke through the fog.

A few weeks earlier I had arrived at a shoot for *20/20* on a Saturday afternoon drunk. (I was always sure, when telling this story, to include that this happened on a *Saturday* afternoon, as if it was somehow slightly less egregious because it happened on a weekend.) That morning, I had found myself in that awful cycle—I called it chasing my tail. You wake up, hungover, and the only thing that will make you feel better is to have a little more to drink. It's tricky, though. You have to stop before you get tipsy again, and when you haven't eaten or slept enough, that sweet spot can be elusive.

I missed it by a long shot that Saturday. I showed up to the shoot location, and my producer, waiting for me outside, took one look at me and knew something was wrong. "Are you okay?" he asked, looking at my face with concern in his eyes. I could barely meet his gaze. He knew in an instant I was in no condition to conduct this interview and sent me home. After that, it's a blur. I remember going to the hospital to get some IV rehydration and Ativan to safely detox. My senior producer and good friend Terri was there, and so was a therapist I had been seeing at the time. He had heard about this facility that specialized in treating post-traumatic stress disorder and substance abuse. He agreed with my therapist at Cirque, who thought I needed help dealing with old childhood trauma—daily panic attacks when my father was at war, the years of bullying, the anxiety and fear that had infused every waking moment. So before I had even fully sobered up, I found myself on a tiny plane, flying to Tennessee.

It was a rough and rude landing when I finally comprehended where I had been sent. I now stood in a shabby little room of a six-bedroom house, watching two staff members rifle through my suitcase.

"This will have to go—no tight tops or tight jeans or yoga pants."

"Why not?" I protest. "I won't have anything to wear."

"You will have to buy loose clothes, or have some sent," they reply. "We have sex addicts at this facility, and women cannot wear anything provocative." I watch half the clothes someone had packed—I guess it was me—tossed into a large plastic garbage bag for storage.

"This cannot go either—no creams or gels allowed in your bathroom. We have people with eating disorders here and they might consume these as a laxative." Into a large Ziploc bag go my Clarins face creams.

"This will have to go, too," a staffer says, waving my electric toothbrush.

I wake up.

"Wait a minute. I have to brush my teeth!!" I say. "You can't take that!"

"You can check it out from this office every morning and every night to brush. But then you have to bring it back here when you are done and check it back in. We have had women who put these where they don't belong and hurt themselves."

I struggle to understand.

"People masturbate with their electric toothbrush,"

they explain. I don't know what I find more startling: someone's desperation for sexual pleasure or their ingenuity.

Once the staff is finished going through every single scrap of clothing and personal hygiene item I have brought along, I am ushered to one of the bedrooms. In it there are two twin beds covered with brown flowered bedspreads. The walls are bare, except for a Smart Board mounted near each of the two dressers.

"You are lucky you have only one roommate," the staffer tells me. There is something vaguely accusatory in her tone. "Most people have to move into the big room next door first—four women in that room. You are supposed to wait for one of the doubles."

I do feel lucky, especially when I meet my roommate, and she is a lovely woman about my age who is neat, like me. Most of the women sharing this house are decades younger. I could be their mother. I sigh and start to unpack the things I have been allowed to keep with me.

Still, I am content to be here and out of the clinic everyone goes to when they first arrive, to detox and wait for a room in one of the houses. That was a grim place, with linoleum floors and fluorescent lights. My first night, I had been sitting on my bed when the door burst open and a woman had barged in, demanding money.

"Do you have any cash? They won't give me my medication. I have to go buy my medication." She was talking too fast, and had started to shout. "I need my fucking *medication*!!"

I had known somehow that I should remain very still, so I had just sat there, hoping someone would hear her and make her leave. Of course I had no money—they had taken all that away from all of us.

The woman finally left and, I later heard, ran out into the night in search of I don't know...a pharmacy? It took hours for the staff to find her in the dark woods and fields surrounding the facility and bring her back.

The building where I was unpacking was one of seven houses, all of them different, collectively known as the Center. We were all grouped loosely by whatever disorder we had come to treat. There was a house for people with eating disorders, another for people with sex addiction, and others for people struggling with drug or alcohol addiction, cutting, depression, and trauma. Women and men were kept strictly apart, at almost all times. The houses were miles from each other, and miles away from the main facility. We were all scattered across the countryside in central Tennessee, about 90 minutes outside Nashville, pretty much in the middle of nowhere.

The majority of our day, it seemed, was spent packed into two white vans that drove up and down a two-lane road, back and forth, to the main center. We piled in for every group session, several times a day, and sometimes when only one of us had a personal session and another ride could not be found. We all had to go, even if we didn't have an appointment. We were not allowed ever to be in the house without at least two staffers present. Thus we all made the trip, twenty minutes each way, creeping or careening around the corners and embankments, depending on which staffer was driving.

I learned the route quickly, like the back of my hand. The first part of the road was unpaved. We bumped along through yawning potholes, leaving an enormous cloud of dust in our wake. The part of the road that was paved curled through the woods, past a shambling creek and a collection of house trailers and abandoned shacks. The twists and turns down the steep hill were stomach churning. There was a broken guardrail where a truck plowed through it and crashed in a ravine below. It sat unrepaired, a silent scold to take it slow.

Much as I hated squeezing into the van over and over every day, it was the only time we got to listen to music—all iPods were banned. Maybe we'd hear an occasional news brief, giving us a glimpse into what was happening in the outside world. Fierce arguments would often break out among the riders over what kind of music to play, and at what volume (earsplitting, or merely deafening). The rule was that whoever sat in the front, shotgun, had to punch up whatever radio station the riders stuck in back decided upon. (One afternoon, when the woman sitting shotgun decided on her own to start changing stations to what she liked, near mutiny broke out.)

Those van rides were also the only brief sojourns in

the outside world. Unlike at Cirque, where physical exercise had been encouraged, there were no daily hikes or bike rides in Tennessee, at least not when I was there in late fall. Twice a week, we could sign up to drive twenty minutes (everything seemed to be twenty minutes away) to the garage of one of the men's houses, in which there were a couple of dusty treadmills and some free weights. There, under the watchful eye of a staff member, you could exercise for half an hour. But more often than not, there wasn't a staff member available to drive us to the "gym," or something else had been planned during that time, so we were unable to go. I tried doing yoga in my bedroom and was reprimanded for it. Eventually a handful of us for whom exercise was important settled on power walking in big circles in the yard around our house, huffing and puffing, looking out for skunk holes. Even then you had to get permission from the staff. If they lost sight of you for even a moment, you would get in trouble.

There were other rules: no TV except on Sunday nights, and no sugar of any kind, also except on Sunday nights. Once a week, we were allowed to bake a cake or make brownies, and we would devour it, inhaling every last crumb. Any baked goods not eaten by ten p.m. would go in the garbage. Coffee was strictly monitored. The staff would prefill some filters each morning and set them on the counter, with just enough grounds in them to turn the water brown. The cans of Folgers were kept in a locked cupboard, alongside the sharp knives.

On one of my first mornings, one of my housemates pulled me aside and showed me how to wait until no one was looking and then pour the grounds of one of the half-filled filters into another, creating a proper serving... and then brew a pot of coffee that actually tasted like real coffee. We all developed a set of signals to each other... raised eyebrows and a slight tilt of your mug meant the pot in there now was a good one. You had to pour a cup quickly though, because at nine a.m. sharp, the staff would dump the contents of all coffeepots into the sink. Coffee hour was over.

We cooked all of our own food. While for breakfast and lunch we were on our own, at dinner we took turns cooking a meal for all fourteen of us, plus the two or three staff members there. I love to cook, but preparing a meal for nearly twenty people is not easy. Whoever's night it was to cook would spend hours that afternoon and evening preparing the meal...chopping, stirring, measuring, hoping the recipe would still work when it was quadrupled. Our tastes ran the gamut. One woman seemed to exist solely on macaroni and cheese and Cheetos. Another woman was so gifted in the kitchen she could whip up an amazing meal out of peanut butter and chicken. I cooked a lot of tofu and brown rice and vegetables. I don't think my meals were the most popular.

We were also assigned chores each week—the most dreaded was garbage duty—and it soon became painfully clear that everyone's idea of what constituted a clean kitchen counter was dramatically different. The dishwashing machine kept breaking down, so on those days a handful of us would spend hours hand washing and drying the dishes left behind by so many people eating three meals a day. The most common conflicts in the house involved accusations that someone wasn't doing their fair share of the work. It's easy to understand why. There were nearly twenty of us—when you include all the staff—stuck inside this house for hours every day. You were never alone except when in the bathroom, and even then someone was often waiting outside for their turn. The effect was claustrophobic.

The days fell into a depressing pattern. Wake up at seven, make breakfast. Morning housekeeping session at eight thirty (where announcements about the day were made), then group therapy session at nine (after a few of us raced upstairs to pour one last cup of coffee). We would then usually pile into the van for another group session down at the main center. Back up the hill to make lunch at eleven thirty. Pile back into the vans for another trip down the hill for more group sessions. Back up the hill to make dinner. Back down the hill for evening sessions. Back up the hill for lights out at ten thirty. It wasn't like this every single day—just most of them. We were each supposed to meet with a private therapist once a week. We could pay extra to meet with one of the Center specialists for trauma work once a week as well.

"I don't understand," I told my therapist one day. "Why am I only seeing you once a week? We are being held here, like captives, or inmates, doing chores and riding in vans all day. I could be doing work with you. This all feels like busywork instead of real work."

My therapist was sympathetic. She tried to meet with me more often, which I think may have been against the rules. She listened as I vented about living with no privacy and guidelines that seemed punitive and infantilizing. Nothing was worse, I told her, than our weekly trips to Walmart. Believe it or not, at the beginning of my stay, it was the highlight of our week, a rare chance to get out and wander the aisles, gazing at the display racks of L'Oreal cosmetics and Pantene hair mousse, dreaming of a life where you needed such things. The trip would last only half an hour, and a staff member waited at the register to monitor what we bought: No caffeine! No soda! No sweets! Another staffer would search our purses and check our receipts upon arrival back at the house.

It didn't stop all the smuggling. Women hid bottles of soda in their coat pockets, bags of Skittles in baggy sleeves, chocolate bars in their bras (you had to get those out fast before they melted). But even these weekly trips were stopped after a man at the Center, in an epic feat of ingenuity, found a way to con a dentist in the nearby town into phoning in a prescription of pain pills to Walmart. He somehow managed to pick them up, pay for them, and get the drugs back to rehab before getting busted. He claimed he was just testing the Center, to see if they would catch him. Right. He quickly became the most hated man at the Center when for nearly a month all trips to Walmart were canceled. When the trips did resume, we were only allowed to go four at a time, walking as a group, with a staff member with us for every moment. It was like being on a toddler rope line...the four of us shuffling along with our minder, first to the dental aisle because someone needed toothpaste, then to the personal hygiene aisle for someone else's Tampax. After that first weekend of renewed privileges, I stopped going.

As I described all this, one therapist asked me how it was that I chose the Center as the place to come get treatment.

"I didn't," I said. "My therapist in New York had heard of this place and thought it would be a good fit."

The staffer shook her head slowly. "I am not sure this is the best place for you," she said. "I would have chosen a different place."

"Well, there is not much I can do about it now," I cried helplessly. And there wasn't. I was stuck. I had to make the best of it.

The bright spot was the bond I formed with several of the other women in the house. There was Janie from Atlanta—who had a big laugh and a warm smile.

We saved seats for each other in the vans. Elaine from Chicago—who was sensitive and wry and funny. Lucy was a talented soccer player who had been through a hellish experience in her teens and was bravely battling her way back. Nicole, who was smart and a trained baker (she was the one who usually baked our cakes Sunday nights) and who was battling a heroin addiction. Melanie was young and beautiful and creative when it came to finding ways to amuse everyone. (One night, on a dare, she put on every single article of clothing she had—and lurched around like the Michelin Man.) One of my closest friends was Lin, a nurse from Philadelphia. She was wise and deep and one of the funniest, most loyal people I have known. I loved my roommate, Frannie, who was there when I first arrived. We would stay up late at night in those first days, talking, telling stories about our lives and how we got here. She was married, and the mother of grown children. She had once been a child actress, and had me gasping with laughter at her stories of growing up on TV sets.

I did not tell her I worked in television. It seemed wrong somehow; I'm not sure why. I went by the name Beth, my childhood name, in rehab, and I wore my hair curly. I didn't think anyone knew who I was, and for some reason I liked it that way.

Then one day we were all crammed into a small hallway, waiting to submit our biweekly urine tests to prove our sobriety, when someone asked me what I did for a living. Everyone got really quiet.

"I'm a writer."

"What kind of writer?"

"I write about news," I hedged.

"What newspaper do you write for?" She was very persistent.

"Well, it's not a newspaper, it's a network. A television network."

There was a long pause. One of the younger women in the back said, "You work for ABC, don't you? You're Elizabeth Vargas."

My stint under the radar was up. I shrugged. "Yes, that's me!" It was actually a relief. The ice was now broken, and I was flooded with questions. I was the newest member to the house; some of these women had been here for months without any idea of what was happening in the outside world. I was suddenly a lifeline.

"Is the government shutdown still happening?"

"Is it true a woman got shot at the Capitol?"

"Did you see the movie *Gravity*?"

"Have you ever interviewed the president?"

"What's Leonardo DiCaprio like? Can you introduce me to him?"

We all laughed, and while I fielded questions for days, it was also good to finally be totally honest about how my lifelong anxiety and insecurity played out for me at work. My inability thus far to manage it in a healthy way was such a big part of my story of addiction. Later that night, as we sat on our beds and sipped our tea, Frannie smiled at me.

"I always knew who you were, you know. I recognized you on the first day. I just wanted to give you your space, until you were ready."

I smiled back. "You really are the best, Frannie."

It was a relief to shed my anonymity to my housemates, but I was horrified when I got a message from ABC News that I was about to be outed to the world. When I had returned to treatment in late October, my bosses at ABC had been incredible, yet again. I was told to take whatever time I needed and to get well. I was so grateful to have that support from Ben Sherwood and James Goldston and Barbara Fedida, and lucky—so many other victims of this disease do not. But this trip to rehab was no longer a secret in the hallways of ABC, or the other networks for that matter. It's very strange, and very public, when the anchor of a national broadcast isn't coming into work. Viewers and competitors must have noticed that David Muir had been solo anchoring *20/20* for several weeks. I was naïve to think no one would write about it. Whatever the backstory, a reporter from the *Daily News* was about to do a story.

I found out when I was pulled out of group session to call Jeffrey Schneider, the executive in charge of publicity, in New York. It was déjà vu—the same conversation with the same person a year and a half ago.

"Hi, Elizabeth, I am so sorry to tell you this, but the *Daily News* is running a report tomorrow saying you are in rehab." For a moment, I couldn't breathe.

Jeffrey, who could not have been nicer or more humane about this, went on.

"The network has to issue a statement, and so should you. We are going to say you are a valued member of the ABC family and we stand by you. But I think you have to tell everyone why you are there."

My most shameful secret was about to be exposed, whether I wanted it or not. With Jeffrey and my therapist at the Center, I wrote out a statement that was released to the press later that day.

"Like so many people, I am dealing with addiction. I realized I was becoming increasingly dependent on alcohol. And feel fortunate to have recognized it for the problem it was becoming. I am in treatment and am so thankful for the love and support of my family, friends, and colleagues at ABC News. Like so many others, I will deal with this challenge one day at a time. If coming forward today gives one other person the courage to seek help, I'm grateful."

Within hours, it was all over the news.

It was very difficult to come out publicly and admit to my alcoholism. I felt deeply ashamed. But no matter how much I was shaken, I had to call my boys before they heard anything from any of their friends at school. My sons knew where I was. To my knowledge, none of their friends did. I was allowed to make one phone call to them after they got out of school. Just as I had done so many times before going on the air, I focused and calmed myself. "They must not hear how upset you are," I told myself.

I got them both on the line.

"I just want to let you know that tomorrow there might be a story in the newspapers about me." They were both still too young to be on the computer, where a headline about their alcoholic mommy might pop up.

Sam asked "What kind of story?"

"It will probably say that I'm here in Tennessee, getting better with a lot of other people who have the same problem I do."

"Why is that going to be in the newspaper?" Zachary puzzled.

"Well, you know...Mommy's on TV and they like to write stories about people who are on TV sometimes. So, if anybody asks you about it at school, you can just tell them, yeah, my mom's getting all better in Tennessee and she'll be home soon."

I wish that first part had been true. I wasn't getting better at the Center. Unlike my stay at Cirque eighteen months earlier, in Tennessee I was completely cut off from Marc and the boys, and it left me absolutely bereft... unable to focus or be present because I was spinning out with worry. There were no nightly Skype sessions here, where I could see Zachary and Sam, and where Marc was supportive.

In Tennessee we were allowed twenty minutes each day to make phone calls, and those calls could only happen between five thirty and seven thirty in the evening Central Time (six thirty to eight thirty in New York). A sheet of paper was put out each day for us to sign up for time slots, but that happened in a haphazard manner. Different staffers would put it out at different times, and no one knew when that might be. If you didn't happen to be standing right there when the sheet went out, you could miss it along with phone privileges that night.

My children went to bed at eight p.m., so I was frantic each day to try to get a slot in the first hour. On the days I lucked out, it was still excruciating. One house phone was in the living room, which was usually full of people talking, the other was in the kitchen with all the clanging of pots and pans as a meal was being prepared. I would hunch over the receiver, one hand pressed against my ear in a vain attempt to muffle the voices around me…my eyes closed, trying to imagine my sons on the other line in our warm kitchen with its bright lights and big bulletin board, crowded with family photos of us in happier times.

"Hi, sweetie! It's Mommy! How are you?" I would try to sound normal and upbeat, and to keep the aching loneliness and desperation for some connection out of my voice. *Sponge Bob* was often playing in the background, competing for their attention.

"Honey, can you turn the TV off for just a minute? I don't have long to talk." It was painful. They were just kids, trying to live their lives and be okay even though their mommy was away in rehab.

"How was school? What did you do after, did you play basketball? Is it cold there?"

Conversations with Marc were harder. He was angry, and justifiably so. He had had it with everything I had put him and our family through for years now. His fury burned through the phone line. Nothing I could say could make it better; no apology was enough. I would hang up after the few times I talked to him, shaking and usually in tears. When I had left New York to come to Tennessee, Marc had promised me he would visit. He had a concert in Nashville two weeks after I checked into the Center, and another in Memphis a day or two later. He actually drove past the rehab on his way there. He did not stop to see his wife, nor did he bring the children for their promised visit. He did not come for family weekend at the Center, when all my other housemates' husbands and loved ones arrived and took part in the family recovery process. He did not write. He could not call. I felt utterly and completely alone. All my old issues of abandonment— memories of my stricken six-year-old self, begging and pleading with my mother not to go to work—took over.

I see-sawed between rage and anguish. On the one hand, I was paying enough attention to what I was hear- ing in rehab to know how destructive it is to punish and shame the alcoholic, who truly suffers from a disease. And, on the other, I was learning that I had to own and accept responsibility for all the terrible things that I had done while drinking—no excuses. I desperately wanted to make things right, but I could not let go of the pain and panic I felt from being so alone.

I simply had to get home. I had to see what had become of my family, what was left of my life. I did and said whatever I could to get out of the Center after 28 days, horribly unaware that I was still fully in the grip of my disease.

—ɷ—

When you're going through hell, keep going.
                    —WINSTON CHURCHILL

I fucked up. There really is no other way to put it. It's profane, and my mother won't like the language, but what I did was profane. I came home, and I drank. Again. I hurt my children, whom I adore, again. I hurt and enraged Marc yet again. Why on earth would I do this? Why would I risk everything, undoing all I had accomplished? All I can guess is that I was not yet ready to stop. I did not yet know how to live my life without numbing myself. I was not yet ready to do anything, to go to any lengths, to stay sober. If that sounds insane after everything I had been through and that I was putting my family through, well it is. It was insane. And selfish.

Within four days, I was back on an airplane, heading back to Tennessee.

I cried and pleaded not to be sent back. I made promises that no one, not even I, believed I could keep. But Marc made it clear I had no choice, and he was right.

He took the boys and left for a concert upstate. I was alone, at home, and I probably would not have made that flight had it not been for my producer and friend, Terri Lichstein, and my brother, Chris. He flew out from San Francisco to be with me. He was gentle and loving. In that moment when I hated myself so much for what I was doing—and felt so hopeless about my inability to stop—my brother was a godsend. He was firm and calm. Chris and Terri insisted I go back, that I must return to the Center, and try harder this time to make it work. Chris flew with me back to Nashville. When the plane landed he was supposed to put me in a car to the Center and head back home to California. But he couldn't bear to do it. He rode with me to the rehab, sitting in the backseat with me, rubbing my arms and my back, comforting me.

I don't think I had ever felt closer to him. And while it was my brother who saved me that day, my sister and my mom and dad also surrounded me with their love and support over the next months. They stepped into the void. I could not have survived without them.

I returned to the Center with my tail between my legs. Early on, one of the administrators at the Center called me in for a meeting. We sat together in a small room. He was about my age, and he looked at me levelly before he started speaking.

"I used to be a judge here in Tennessee," he said. "I had a huge, promising career as a lawyer, a wife and kids.

I had it all, and then I nearly lost it because I couldn't stop drinking."

I studied him. He seemed so put together, so calm, even serene, as he told me his terrible story. He seemed free of all the guilt and shame I felt crowding around me.

"I am a drunk, Elizabeth, and so are you." I recoiled. His words felt like a slap in the face. "You may think you're special, or different, but you're not. You are just like me, and every other person here, trying to stay sober." I started to cry. He continued. "You need to take this chance and make the best of it. Many, many people relapse. You are not the first, and you will not be the last. The question is what are you going to do about it."

He was right, on so many levels. I was not the first person in the world to leave rehab and drink—not by a long shot. But I felt like I was. And now, I was right back in the same house, living under the same strict rules, feeling just as despondent and isolated as ever. I knew that this time I had to fight to save my life.

One of the first things I did was to try to alleviate the yawning abandonment I felt by being at the Center. I could not make it go completely away, but I began reaching out to people who would support me and talk to me: my parents, my brother, my sister, and my friends Dana and Michelle. I figured out that I could call my own work voice mail and access messages from that living room phone at the Center. I asked everyone to leave word for me on it. I could call it every night, if I made it to the phone sign-up sheet in time, and in five minutes I could hear what felt like a week's worth of love and encouragement.

My mom in particular left a message almost every single night. Echoes of those lunch box notes she would give me in third grade when I was tormented at school by the class bully. My priority still was calling Zachary and Sam, trying as best I could to connect with them, and that took most of my allotted phone time. But those other messages now left me better equipped to handle the heartbreak of the calls home.

One night, as I sat listening to my messages, I heard an unfamiliar voice. It was a friend of my sister's. She was in recovery. Aimie had given her my number.

"Elizabeeeeeeeethh! How are you? Hang in there! But hey, don't you know? *Getting* sober is so much harder than *staying* sober. Why do you keep doing the hardest part over and over?"

I had never looked at it that way. I have thought about that message almost every day since I heard it. Why had I stayed in that terrible spin cycle, over and over, emerging battered and disoriented, and then climbing back in for another go? Quitting is so very hard. "I'll stop tomorrow" is the worn-out refrain. But it feels herculean to resist drinking on day one. It's only once you have days, weeks, or months of sobriety under your belt that the siren call to drink is much less potent. It is easier to reject the temptation to drink if your mind is clear and you're not hungover or feeling hopeless because you drank the night before.

I worked hard with my therapist at the Center, trying to solve the mystery of why I kept going back to what was killing me. Once again, we dug deep into why my anxiety was so terrifying to me, and how I could calm it without wine. I listened to lecturers explain that alcoholism is a disease of the mind *and* body...that alcoholics cannot stop drinking or obsessing about it once they start. I went to the Center's trauma expert, who did something called brain spotting. I had to sit and stare at the tip of a stick that the therapist would slowly wave back and forth. When she explained it to me, I burst into a laugh.

"You're kidding me, right?"

The trauma therapist looked annoyed and mildly offended. "No, I am not kidding you. Are you ready to work or not?"

Yes, I was ready to work. She made me tell her about those mornings in Okinawa—when my dad was in Vietnam and my mom left for work. She made me describe in detail how I clung to her, begged her, was dragged to the car trying to stop her, my bare feet skidding across the rocks. I could barely tell anyone that story. Every time I started I would become overwhelmed, and have to stop. At that point, the therapist made me stare at that silly stick again, and she moved it slowly from side to side. I had to keep my head still, following it only with my eyes moving.

I honestly have no idea what she was doing or how it was supposed to work, but unbelievably, after several sessions, it did work. For the first time in my whole life, I can now tell the story of those panic attacks in Okinawa without crying.

There were other exercises, meant to build our trust in the world and in ourselves, and to make us believe that we could be okay. We were all led out to a small cliff one afternoon, high above a gully full of dead trees and rocks. One by one, we were strapped into a harness and told to stand on the very edge of the cliff and jump.

We all knew we wouldn't fall—that's what the harness and the safety ropes above were for—but trust me, it was scary. Because I am afraid of heights, I volunteered to go first. Why sit and wait and worry—just get it over with. I forced myself to look down. I wanted to feel fully afraid, and then I held my breath and jumped. For one second, the world, the trees, even I, all felt suspended in time, like a scene from the movie *The Matrix*. For a nanosecond it felt like I floated, and then I plummeted, my stomach lurching up into my throat. And then with a jerk, I stopped, swinging gently in my safety harness, laughing up at the sky.

My therapist also taught me how to meditate. She took Lin, Elaine, and me to Nashville one Saturday for a day-long silent retreat. No talking, just meditating.

"I don't think I can do it," Elaine said from the backseat of the van. "What happens if we blurt out something? Are they going to kick us out?"

"I have never not talked for a whole day in my life!" Lin exclaimed. "This is epic!" We were giddy, mostly just to be allowed out of the Center for a day.

We were on our way to the gorgeous Vanderbilt campus, where one of our first exercises was a walking meditation. We all had to walk, very, very slowly, repeating one line of the mantra with each step:

May I be calm.
May I be peaceful.
May I be happy.
May I be healthy.

I put one foot out carefully in front of the other, so slowly I was barely moving. Lin and Elaine and I tried not to look at each other. We might start giggling. We felt like zombies, moving slowly and muttering chants to ourselves. But to my surprise, I liked it. We spent the day learning all kinds of meditation—standing, seated, with a mantra, and without.

I learned that day that I loved to meditate. It was the first time ever that I had been able to calm my anxiety without a drink or even a pill. Meditating would go on to become a key part of my recovery.

But the best part of the Center's recovery program, in my opinion, is when they have family weekends. Once or twice a month, everyone's husband or wife, children, parents, and siblings are invited to come to the Center and spend three days, learning about addiction and that it is a family disease. While the family has most certainly been profoundly hurt by the addict's actions, the Center therapists said, blaming and shaming the addict is the worst possible thing a family can do. Many alcoholics also drink because of deep dysfunction in families, and for the family to heal, every member of the family must recognize his or her part. On the last day of the family weekend, the addicts and their family members were to read to each other a list of regrets and requests. This was done in front of a group, with everyone else watching. It was an important and emotional part of the weekend.

"Now, family members," warned Teddy, the program leader. "This is not your chance to blame the alcoholic for every bad thing that has ever happened! You don't get to write 'I regret that you drank.' It has to be something you did. You can request they don't drink. But you have to own your own failures. Like, 'I regret I didn't listen to you when you tried to tell me you were unhappy,' or 'I regret I got defensive and lashed out at you when you tried to tell me what was wrong.'"

Teddy was a character. He was a strapping man with a booming voice and a thick southern accent, and I think he lulled everyone into thinking he was a good ol' boy. He was actually whip smart and could charm just about anyone to drop their defenses and listen. He was also a recovering alcoholic.

Hoping he would come and hear what Teddy had to

say, I invited Marc to every family weekend. He never came. But my parents did—all the way from Reno. So did my brother, Chris. Aimie would have come, but she is a single mother with three young children and couldn't. Even my friend Dana offered to come from Los Angeles.

Chris came first. We sat opposite each other in chairs, our list of regrets and requests in our laps.

"I regret I was not there for you more when we were growing up," Chris said.

"I regret I didn't ask you more about what was happening in your life."

"I request that you stop drinking." Then, Chris put down the paper and looked up at me.

"You light up a room when you walk into it, Beth. Don't walk into it drunk."

I started to cry. I picked up my paper and read what I had written.

"I regret that I hurt you. I regret that I let you and Mom and Dad and Aimie slip away from me."

"I regret not asking you about your new business. I know it's important to you, and I regret hurting you with my disinterest."

"I regret that I didn't tell you what was happening to me, how I was losing myself. I regret not asking for help. I didn't when we were little and I was so scared (and you must have been, too), and I didn't when we were grown up and could do something about it."

"I request you call me more."

"I request we try harder to stay closer."

Exchanging those regrets and requests, first with my brother and, later, with my parents, helped clear out some of the emotional clutter that had for years kept me and my family from truly talking. When my mother sat across from me and told me she regretted that she did not comfort me in Okinawa, and that she did not stop the bullies from tormenting me for years, it was like an enormous weight was lifted from me. Her simple statement that she knew what I had gone through, and was sorry she didn't do more, somehow eased the pain of those 40-year-old memories that I had been dragging behind me all my life, like bedraggled baggage.

Everything was on the table that weekend for everyone to explore. We drew an enormous family tree, labeling any ancestors who were alcoholic or depressed and any relatives who experienced trauma of any kind. Addicts are rarely spawned in a vacuum.

Each family weekend ended with a maze made of ropes. I went through it with Chris. We put on blindfolds and were led to a large room, which contained a series of ropes. We would have to feel our way along the ropes to find the exit.

"The rules are very simple!" Teddy boomed. "Do not let go of the rope! Do not duck under the rope! Do not climb over the rope! Do not try to walk on top of the rope! [*Seriously?*] Feel along the rope with your hands until you find the way out!"

We all looked at each other uneasily, some smiling, others searching around for a way out of doing this.

"If you have a question, or you need something, raise your hand!! One of us will come to you. *Do you understand?*" Teddy was especially thunderous on maze days.

Cue the music, don the blindfolds, and off we went. Shuffling and bumping, we were led into a large space, and our hands first touched a rope. We groped along. The ropes were stretched in what seemed to be a giant cat's cradle. Chris and I were in the crowd, fumbling around, when suddenly Teddy shouted, "Ladies and gentlemen, we welcome our first person home!"

There was applause from the staffers and residents watching. *Wow*, I thought. *Someone did it!* On and on I went, bumping into people, walking into walls. I could hear people swearing around me as they did the same thing. Teddy kept yelling every few minutes, "We welcome another person home!!" and then there was more applause for whoever figured the way out. I was beginning to feel frustrated, like I was going around in circles. How could all these other people find the way out and I could not? It was annoying to hear all that clapping as yet another person succeeded while I was still looking. I forced myself to focus. Think. Use your head. Count how many steps before turning left, stop, the wall is on the right, it must be forward. Finally, after walking into my fifteenth wall, it occurred to me. I raised my hand. Moments later I felt Teddy's hand on my back. "Do you need anything?" he asked.

"Yes, I need help." That, ladies and gentlemen, was the way out of the maze. The way out of alcoholism, the way out of any crisis. Asking for help. "No one can do it alone," Teddy said, as my brother and my housemates gathered around me (they had all figured it out long before I did). "We all need help. We can't think our way out of addiction. We can't will our way out. The first step to recovery is raising your hand and asking for help."

—⚏—

Unhappy Holidays

Christmas Eve, 2013. I am sitting in the living room window of the crowded house at the Center, watching the taillights of the last staffer to leave dissolve into the night fog. I am struck by a memory—sitting in my living room window in Stuttgart, Germany, watching the taillights of my parents' car recede as they drove away for a week's vacation. I feel a little of that terrible panic from that day decades ago... how could they leave me? Would they ever come back?

I usually love Christmas, but this year it is unbearable. We are all stuck inside. A misting rain clings to the tree branches and the eaves, droplets quivering, before falling to the sodden wooden deck below. My parents and my sister have both sent me gifts—a few books, body lotion, and some homemade gingerbread cookies. The cookies and the lotion are both confiscated. "Against the rules," says the staffer as she tosses them onto a shelf. I wince. Those little things mean the world to me. They are all I have this year. My nieces and nephews have all sent drawings of Santa Claus and Christmas trees. I hang them in my bedroom, next to my pictures of Zach and Sam, and I lay on my bed and wonder what my children are doing at that exact moment. I could not get much information from them on the phone. And I couldn't yet tell them when I would be home. Marc was insisting I stay until the therapists at the Center cleared me to leave. That date had finally been settled—for the second week of January. Now he was insisting I stay even longer. I felt like he was trying to whitewash me out of our life back in New York.

New Year's Eve was slightly better than Christmas, mostly because I was now counting the days until I would go back to New York. Since it was a holiday, we were allowed to watch movies. *Pitch Perfect* was playing for the fourth time since I had been there, so I wandered into the kitchen and waited for my turn on the phone. The boys answered when I called.

"Happy New Year, you guys!! Happy New Year! What are you doing that's special tonight?"

"Hi, Mommy! We are staying up until midnight!!"

"Midnight!? Oh my gosh, that's so late!" I said. "Are you going to watch the New Year's Eve Times Square show?"

"Yeah, but maybe a movie first. We're having dinner now." At that point I heard Bev, our nanny, call Sam to the table to eat.

"What's Bev doing there tonight?"

"Daddy's going out. He's getting all dressed up right now."

"Huh." I was taken aback. "Can I talk to Dad?"

"Sure—bye, Mommy!" I could hear Sam yelling, "Dad, pick up the phone!"

"Hello?" It was Marc.

"Hi. Happy New Year."

"Happy New Year to you." He was curt, overly formal.

"The boys said you were getting all dressed up. Where are you going?"

"I'm going out to dinner," he answered.

"With who?" My question was honestly innocent. It had never occurred to me to be jealous.

"That's none of your business!" he snapped. "I don't know what *you* are doing on New Year's Eve; you don't have any right to ask me what I am doing!"

I was stunned, completely taken aback. "What do you mean?" I stammered. "You know exactly what I am doing tonight. I am locked up in rehab."

I can't even remember how the conversation ended. It certainly wasn't with any wishes that 2014 be better than the last few years, or pledges to work together to at least try to heal our fractured marriage. I just remember hanging up the phone feeling shaken and absolutely certain in my core that something was very wrong.

—∿—

Center Stage, Whether
I Liked It or Not

The first days of the new year, my final days at the Center, were mired in negotiations with Marc about coming home. He had finally brought the boys to Tennessee, not for the long promised visit, but because a therapist he was consulting told him they should see me before I arrived home in a few days. The Center had cleared me to return January 13th, but that date happened to fall while Marc was out of town. He wanted me to stay in Tennessee until he got home. Given what happened the last time I got out of rehab, I understood his request. But I argued that I was ready to come home, and to sit around in rehab doing nothing was ridiculous. I was paying for all this myself, along with all the bills in our household, while I was away. The financial burden was becoming a strain. So I agreed to sleep at my friend Michelle's apartment for ten days until Marc came back to town.

It was absolutely wonderful to come home. I hugged my sons long and hard, thrilled to see them, to feel them in my arms. I unpacked my suitcases and tossed all those loose-fitting clothes in the wash. I wandered around my apartment. I never felt luckier to live there. I spent all the afternoons and evenings with the boys after school, helping with homework, cooking their dinner, and putting them to bed, before heading over to Michelle's to sleep. I didn't allow myself even a whiff of resentment at the arrangement.

Besides, I loved sleeping at Michelle's. Her spare bedroom was in the back—facing a courtyard. It was dark and quiet, and I slept longer and harder than I ever had. I luxuriated in her big bed with its plump pillows and crisp sheets.

I was exhausted and bone weary from all those months in a twin bed, in a crowded house, rising at seven a.m. I slept in until ten or eleven every day that first week, for the first time in twenty years...maybe more. By that time, Michelle had gone to work. I'd rub the sleep from my eyes and pour myself a bracingly strong cup of coffee, lingering over a second cup, treasuring the solitude and the quiet after three months of communal living.

I felt like someone who had been sealed away for a very long time and had just returned to life. I got my hair cut and my nails done for the first time in three months. It felt like the best manicure and blowout I had ever had. I drank green juice and ate sushi. It never tasted so good. In the hours before picking up the boys from school, I read newspapers and watched CNN, starved for information about the world and what had happened while I was gone. I was like Rip Van Winkle, emerging from a long sleep and discovering that my old life felt brand-new again.

Most important, every day I met with other alcoholics, to keep my recovery going strong. I also joined an outpatient group at a recovery center, and I met there three days a week. I stayed in close touch with my therapist back at the Center, and with my friends Lin and Janie from Tennessee who were also now home. I was determined that this time, I would succeed.

I returned to work at ABC while Marc was still away. I was nervous. The whole world now knew my dirty little secret, and as I rode up the elevator on my first day back, I was afraid to meet people's gazes. It was strange, walking the hallway to my office, like it was any other day, like my wine-soaked meltdowns and three months in rehab never happened. My heart was thumping in my chest. I was afraid people would shun me, that everyone was thinking, "Oh look who's back—*20/20*'s resident lush."

But the people who tapped on the door to say welcome back or give me a quick hug were wonderful and empathic. Maybe they already knew what was true: that behind our carefully contrived exteriors, we all have something we're dealing with. No one walks through the world immune to insecurity, worry, failure, heartbreak. It was just that all of mine had been laid out for everyone to see.

It was only a few hours into that first day when there came a tap on the door. It was Jeff Schneider. He gave me a warm smile and a big hug, and then shook his head ruefully.

"Darlin', I hate to do this, but Page Six just called. They heard you were back to work today and are going to run a story." My heart sank. No one outside ABC knew when I was returning. Someone at the network must have called in the tip.

I sighed.

"What do you want me to say?" Jeffrey asked. We came up with a brief statement saying I was indeed home, back at work, and grateful to be there. We both knew we could not let the drip-drip-drip of stories continue. Piecemeal statements in response to tips—"Yes I am an alcoholic. Yes I am home from rehab. Yes I am back to work."—were only fanning the buzz and the interest. I was inundated with requests for interviews from talk show hosts and magazines.

"The best thing you can do now is pick someone, sit down, and tell them everything," Jeffrey advised.

It's the first lesson of damage control: tell the truth, tell it all, and put it past you. Hedging, delaying, hiding, and denying will just drag a story out. Better to get it out early and completely. I already knew that and had planned on eventually doing an interview, but not now. I had just come home. I wasn't ready.

"The stories will just continue," Jeffrey warned. "Put it to bed." So that day, my first day back at work, we began making arrangements to do a tell-all sit-down interview.

Initially, the plan was just to air it on *GMA*, the show I had been hosting as I filled in for Robin, just one year before. I picked George Stephanopoulos, with whom I had shared the anchor desk over the years for hundreds of hours of live television. I knew he was tough but fair, and he had integrity. He would ask hard questions, but I trusted him.

The arrangements were made to tape the interview that Thursday. It would air Friday morning.

At nine thirty a.m. on January 23, I arrived at the *GMA* studios in Times Square and sat down opposite George. As we had countless times before, we both pinned tiny microphones to our clothes while the crews adjusted the focus on their cameras and checked the enormous lights around us. This time, only he had some papers in his lap, a list of questions and notes he had jotted down. I arrived to the studio empty-handed. It felt very, very different to be the subject of the story instead of the journalist reporting it.

For the first time I really understood why nearly everyone I interviewed confessed they were nervous to be on camera. I was terrified. My heart was pounding; my hands were cold and clammy. I felt distracted by my own anxiety, by the sensation of being completely out of control of the next twenty minutes. I was unable to make any small talk with the people around me, people with whom I had worked a thousand times. As the makeup artist powdered my shiny forehead I wondered yet again, *Is this the right thing to do?*

"Are you ready?" George asked. I nodded and took a deep breath. I had no idea what he was going to ask. I had no idea what I was going to say. All I knew was that I had to be honest.

G: So, you're an alcoholic.

I nearly died. *You're going to start with that question? The hardest question, right out of the box?* For a moment, I thought about stopping the interview, asking for some time to warm up, some space to compose myself. Then I swallowed and said,

E: I am. I am an alcoholic. It took me a long time to admit that to myself. It took me a long time to admit it to my family, but I am.

Okay—it was out there.

G: And it must have taken so much effort to keep that secret.

E: The amount of energy I expended keeping that secret and keeping this problem hidden from view, hidden from my family, hidden from friends, from colleagues, was exhausting.

George's face was compassionate, and yet his expression was baffled.

G: I mean, you and I have spent literally hundreds of hours this far apart anchoring live television. I would have never guessed this in a million years.

E: I mean, George, it's a staggering burden to walk around with. And you become so isolated with the secret and so lonely because you can't tell anyone what's happening. And yet it was a fact of my life. I spent most of my childhood having almost daily panic attacks and most of my adulthood, um, having a lot of panic and dealing with a lot of severe anxiety. I dealt with that anxiety and with the stress that that anxiety brought by starting to drink.

G: Did anyone close to you realize?

E: My husband. My husband knew I had a problem.

G: What did he say?

E: You have a problem. You're, you're an alcoholic. And, and it made me really angry. Really angry. But he was right.

G: So when Marc first said something to you, did you immediately go and seek professional help, go to rehab?

E: No. It took a long time. I mean, denial is huge for any alcoholic, especially for any functioning alcoholic, um, because I, you know, I'm not living under a bridge. I haven't been arrested.

No arrests. Just a bunch of other really horrible things, like waking up in an emergency room after a thirteen-hour blackout.

E: I had a panic attack on live television when I was anchoring the local news in Chicago. I had to take beta blockers because I was so nervous and so anxious and, and you know, that's exhausting to, to live like that. And it becomes very easy to think, I deserve this glass of wine. I'm so stressed out, and I'm keeping it hidden. I can't tell anybody, not even you, sitting next to me...I felt like I had to be, you know, perfect, which is ridiculous. Um, nobody's perfect.

Except I thought I had to be. All the while I was failing miserably.

G: So what happened?

E: I went to a rehab that specializes in treating trauma.

G: How long did you stay?

E: I—I stayed for twenty-eight days and left against their advice and came home because I really wanted to come home. And they said, we think you need to do more work, and I came home for five days and realized they were right, and I went back and finished and stayed until the doctors there said I was ready to come back. Um, and I, you know, this isn't what I want to be known for, um, but I'm really proud of what I did.

G: How did you know you were ready to come back, to come home?

E: You know, it's, it's a psychic change, I think. I mean, it's learning to accept that I'm human, that there's nothing wrong with failing, that there's nothing wrong with feeling anxiety.

Anxiety can't kill you, even when it feels like it can.

G: Marc must be relieved too.

To be honest, I don't really know. I haven't seen him yet.

E: Yes. And my kids. You know, my kids, too.
G: Is it hard not to drink?
E: Yes.

George looks surprised. People who don't have this disease really don't fully understand the need to blot out the feeling that I don't quite fit into this skin . . . the need for immediate relief.

E: Right now, I feel really strong, and I've got a great support system in place. I have great, great friends who, um, who I love and who love me.
G: What are your triggers? What are the stress points?
E: Daily stress. Listen, there are lots of people who feel a lot of stress. Not everybody turns to a glass of wine or three like I did, or four, like I did on some occasions. What I learned to do when I was away was to feel the feelings. You know what? They're

not gonna kill you. You have to experience them, and I never learned that skill and it makes it tough some days. Alcohol, for me, is no longer an option.

G: Well, what are the tricks now? So when you feel that, what do you do instead?

E: Call a friend. Um, meditate. Pray. There's been a real spiritual component for me in all of this. Reach out to somebody who can talk you through that rotten day and support you in that.

I hate talking about myself like this. I feel naked in front of the world.

G: Telling your story, sharing it now, do you think it makes a difference in how you live your life?

E: It's always embarrassing to have the entire world know your deepest, darkest secret and yet, I think in the long term it will be, ultimately, a blessing because I can be free about it.

Ultimately. Not quite yet.

G: Well, you look great and you sound great. Are you ready to get back to work?

E: I feel great. I am! [*laughs*] I'm really ready to get back to work.

G: Welcome back.

George could not have been nicer. I thanked the crew and left the interview suite in a bit of a daze. My legs felt wobbly. I felt like I had just run ten miles. Later that day, I learned the segment would run for seven minutes on *GMA*...twice as long as the time originally allotted for it. I could not remember ever doing a segment on the show that ran as long.

Friday morning, I woke up early at Michelle's, poured myself some coffee, and curled up on the couch to watch. I was gripping my mug with both hands, afraid I would spill it. *What if I sound ridiculous? What if I sound defensive? What if the interview is edited in a weird way and I don't make sense? What if I look as sweaty and nervous as I felt?*

But before I could spin out any further, Robin and George were introducing the story, and moments later, my face loomed in the screen stating, for all the world to hear, "I am an alcoholic."

I wondered, in that moment, about all the people in my life who I had not yet had the chance to tell...people who might be shocked, or who might say, "I always knew." I wondered if my husband was watching it somewhere, in a hotel room, on the road, and what he thought of my long-overdue, televised admission.

It was excruciating to watch, but I did it, and when it was over, the response was enormous. I was flooded with calls and emails from friends and colleagues; I received letters from people all over the country—wishing me luck, praising my courage, sharing their own battles with addiction.

My *20/20* co-host, David Muir—who had been one of the most supportive people at the network the whole time I was in rehab—decided to do a story about me for our show, using parts of my interview, along with new interviews with my mother and my friends. As I stood on the set with David my first night back, he warmly welcomed me. I was able to fully take in how lucky and happy I was to have this job. But I knew harder days were ahead. Marc was coming home. I had a lot of work to atone for everything I had put him through with my drinking, and to try to save our marriage.

In my final days in Tennessee they had told me, over and over, do not make any big life changes in your first year of recovery. Your sobriety is too new, too fragile. All the ordinary feelings you have been numbing with alcohol can seem overwhelming. It's advice every addict hears. I, however, never had the chance to take it.

—⚉—

The wheel of life takes one up and down by turn.

—KALIDASA

I am perched on the edge of my bed and my husband is sitting on the floor in front of me, his legs crossed, his voice low and calm. I cannot feel my body, and my face feels numb. "I have feelings for someone else," he tells me. "We want to explore being together." I am shocked, reeling, as I struggle to process what he is saying. My mind feels—well, it feels drunk. Drunk and clumsy. Like I am underwater, moving in slow motion, trying to fit pieces into a puzzle, but the pieces keep floating away and I am too slow to grasp them and put them where they belong.

Too soon, the warning not to make big life decisions feels quaint. Life has outpaced me. Just days after moving back into my apartment, my husband told me he wanted a divorce. Weeks after unpacking my cheerful cards from my housemates and my books of daily reflections, I learned Marc had been sharing holidays and intimate dinners with another woman...a woman I had introduced him to, a woman I had thought was my friend. While I was away in Tennessee, Marc had hired a divorce lawyer and started legal proceedings.

I sit there in my nightgown, unable to say a word, even as the pieces finally thud into place—his refusal to come to any family weekend, his fury when I asked where he was going New Year's Eve—and still, I cannot believe it. I look down at my hands and I realize they are shaking. Our children are asleep in the next room, and it is all coming to an end. This. Our life together. Our marriage. I had thought when he first mentioned a divorce that he was just angry. He had every right to be. I had hurt him so very much. But hearing him talk about this other woman and their feelings for each other left no doubt in my mind: Marc had moved on.

In the days, weeks, and months that followed, I seesawed between disbelief and fury. Without alcohol, the pain was brittle, sharp-edged. While I didn't yearn for the hazy soft-edged fog of wine, I needed something to escape the pain, or at least dull it. I spent hours cleaning closets, organizing cabinets, cooking, baking—anything to try to divert and distract me from the cyclone of questions: *How could this really be happening? How can I fix this?* I kept banging into the same wall, the one that has "you're not in control anymore" spray-painted on it.

I clung to my new sobriety like a life raft. I went to meetings with other alcoholics and raged about my crumbling life, sharing how seared I felt by the rejection, but nothing could blunt it or alter the course of events. By May, Marc had found a new apartment and bought himself new furniture, and at the end of the month he moved out and on to his new life. Left behind were closets crammed with his clothes and guitar cases, shelves filled with photos of birthdays and beach vacations...all no longer wanted or needed, shed like an old skin. He had a clean slate, with no reminders of the past. I was confronted with the memories and the wreckage every time I opened a drawer.

We all learned to navigate our new reality and the painful new routines: the walks with Zachary and Sam to Daddy's new house, the awkward pickups after school with other parents' pitying smiles, the dropoffs on the nights the boys were sleeping with him—their empty beds and the screaming silence in my home. I didn't know what to do with myself those nights. I would wander around the apartment, straightening photographs, picking up toys and socks they had left lying on the floor. It was physical, this ache I had for them. I still could not believe this was how life was going to be.

It was summer when it all began to fall apart for me. I don't know exactly what it was that pushed me over the edge, sent me tumbling back into the swamp of addiction. Was it another long weekend without the boys? News from my divorce lawyer that as the "moneyed spouse" I would have to pay for Marc's lawyer, too? Someone thoughtlessly tattling that they had seen Marc strolling up Broadway holding hands with another brunette?

Maybe it was just everything—the fighting, the worry, the financial strain of supporting two households—it was all pressing down, too hard. At some point the misery of those months in Tennessee and the memory of what drinking had done to me was eclipsed by my daily distress. I forgot to meditate and pray—they seemed like flimsy weapons in this battle. I forgot what I had told George in that *GMA* interview—that my feelings couldn't kill me. I felt like I was dying of grief. I would do anything not to feel that. And I did. A few times that summer, I did what I swore I would never again do: I drank. It was just a handful of times, but it was enough to set me on a terrible course as August, and my first vacation as a single parent with my boys, loomed.

—〰—

Half measures availed us nothing. We stood at the turning point.

—Alcoholics Anonymous

I hit bottom on August 16, 2014. It was Sam's birthday. I had rented a beautiful house in the week leading up to it, on the beach in Malibu. It had wraparound decks and stunning views of the waves roaring and crashing just below. I had planned this trip for two months, my first ever vacation trip with just my two sons.

I had wanted these ten days at the beach to be a balm, a salve to all our pain. I had wanted us to be happy even though we were now three instead of four. Looking back, I shudder at how high I pinned my hopes for this trip: how much I wanted to erase all the pain and heartbreak and loss and betrayal I had felt, and had inflicted on my children. What I should have done was steel myself for the hard times that would also come far away from home, even in paradise.

For Sam's birthday, I had carefully selected an iPad

Mini and wrapped it in shiny gold paper. I had planned to bake him a vanilla coconut cake, his favorite, and had bought eight blue candles—and a red one for luck—to put on top. But on that bright sunny Saturday, with the salt from the ocean thick in the air, eight years after I brought my freckle-faced redhead into this world, I was drunk. I was upstairs, throwing all my clothes into my suitcases. The dresses I had planned to wear to dinner with friends, the bathing suits I packed to surf with the boys, the flip-flops, the sandals, the sun hats, the cashmere wraps—all the things I meticulously laid out six days ago, I now shoved back in with abandon. Downstairs, my friend Dana loaded the boys into her car to take them to her house to play with her daughters while they waited for Marc to fly from New York to pick them up. My brother, Chris, who had flown down from San Francisco with my sister, to save me yet again, waited to drive me to a detox facility in Pasadena.

In two short hours I traded those thousand-dollar views of the Pacific Ocean for a tiny room in a Las Encinas lockup. I had a single bed and a small window that was bolted shut. There was no door to the tiny bathroom, no hooks on which to hang towels out of fear that someone would try to hang themselves. There was a single fluorescent overhead light buzzing faintly, and the sharp, cloying smell of industrial detergent.

Every hour, day and night, an orderly would open the door and shine a light to see if you were in your bed (at night) or still breathing (day or night). Once I sobered up, I spent every waking hour outside in a small common courtyard. I was told by one of the staff that this place was once called the Marilyn Monroe Center, because it was here that she would come to privately detox. If true, the place was definitely showing its age.

Outside, where I spent the next four days, there was a collection of picnic benches. Styrofoam cups and used paper plates sat on tables, and in the desiccated grass were cigarette butts... mounds of them. All matches and lighters had been confiscated upon check-in, so hour after hour I sat and watched person after person stand in front of a rusty metal box mounted at eye level on the wall and lean their face in close. Embedded inside it was one of those old-fashioned cigarette lighters, the kind you would see in an old Buick in the 1970s. I was sure one of those smokers was going to ignite his eyelashes instead of his Marlboro Gold. And that is how I spent the week of my son's eighth birthday. Instead of watching Sam blow out his birthday candles, I was watching nameless addicts light up their smokes.

I had plenty of time in those four days in Las Encinas to think about what I did when we arrived in Malibu. I had worked the first day of our vacation, on Monday, shooting an interview for a story that would air that week on *20/20*. I was scheduled to record the audio for my script on Friday, from the house, so it could be fed via satellite to New York and edited into the story. But when the crew arrived to our Malibu rental that day, I was under the influence, unable to properly read the script. A few days before, while shopping for groceries, my cart loaded with fruit and cereal and chips and salsa, I had found myself wheeling it past an enormous display of wine. I stopped in front of it, gazing at all those bottles. *That would make me feel better*, I had thought. *Just one bottle, just one glass tonight.* Then, forgetting every hard lesson I had learned, I reached out and picked a nice California chardonnay.

That night, I drank more than half of that bottle. The following night, after draining it, I looked around the rental house for more. I could not drive to the store again—I had sipped a glass and a half already. I would never dare drive after drinking—a singular moment of lucidity in an otherwise insane episode. I opened every cabinet, searched every shelf. Finally, way in the back of the pantry, next to a container of margarita mix, I found a bottle of tequila. Hard liquor was not my thing, but it was all there was, so I poured myself a glass. The tequila was strong—too strong. Very quickly my head was spinning, and I had to go to my room to lie down. The boys and our nanny were already asleep, thank God, but by Friday, I was hopelessly ensnared…it was clear to everyone that I had relapsed.

This time, my bosses at ABC had had it. The network had stood by me through two lengthy stints in rehab and through two relapses already. This time, I nearly lost my job. But most crucially, I had hurt my children—deeply. As I sat on that picnic bench and watched the smokers light up I wondered bleakly if they would ever forgive me, ever trust me again.

I had two visitors during those four days in Las Encinas—my sister, Aimie, was the first. She flew down a second time from the Bay Area to offer her support and her love.

"Beth, you have got to stop doing this."

"I know, I know," I said miserably. "I have really messed up this time. I may lose everything and everyone."

Aimie looked around the yard, taking in the depressing scene in which I was now a player.

"You have to fight for yourself. This has to be the most important thing you do."

I was deeply grateful she came, and when she left, it was really hard to see her go...her small back, her head held high. She had not had an easy time of life, either—she had had her own painful divorce to go through. She had gone through it without drinking herself into oblivion and, I realized in that moment, had done it without sufficient support from me.

I called out to her as she reached the locked door to the outside world. "Bye, Aimie! I love you!"

She turned and waved. "I love you, too."

My second visitor was someone I had just met on my trip to Malibu. He was an actor and director who had gone through his own highly public battle with alcohol. He had taken me to a meeting in Malibu with other alcoholics, at the beginning of my vacation, before I fell into the bottle. He had come that Friday morning, too, when it all fell apart, and with my brother and Dana had helped get me to this facility. When they talk in recovery about alcoholics helping other alcoholics, this man's name should be at the top of the list. He arrived in Las Encinas on my third day, and he brought someone with him. Her name was Polly.

"Elizabeth, meet Polly. This woman got me sober, and kept me sober. She saved my life."

Polly had big brown eyes, long hair, and a warm smile. She was lovely. "It's nice to meet you!" she said.

The three of us sat down in a pretty, secluded area apart from the common yard—a concession by the staff to my visitor's fame.

"How are you doing?" he asked.

"I am okay," I sighed. They both knew I was lying. They knew exactly how I felt. Hopeless.

The three of us sat and talked for half an hour, Polly telling how she helped our friend get sober, telling me her own story of addiction. She had been sober now for more than twenty years. Her wisdom and her strength awed me.

"You can stay sober, Elizabeth. I have helped many alcoholics who are worse than you." She was offering me a ray of hope I had by then denied myself. "All you have to do is follow some simple steps. If you are willing, I can help you."

She seemed so serene, so sure. As I looked at her that day, I saw my only lifeline. I grabbed it with both hands. By the end of the visit, we came up with a plan. Polly would come home with me to New York and live with me.

I knew going to another rehab was not the answer for me. Instead, this time I resolved to work with Polly every day.

Polly flew home with me two days later and moved into my guest bedroom. I returned to a very different life than the one I left, on my way to Malibu, where I turned that dream vacation into yet another nightmare. I was no longer working. ABC had agreed to give me one last chance to get it together, but this time without pay. I returned to my outpatient group. I slept every night for a month at a sober house, where I was tested daily to prove I had not been drinking. But most important, I worked each and every day with Polly.

She laid out a meticulous timeline of my entire adult life and showed me how I had used alcohol for years in an unhealthy way, almost always to escape something, or someone, usually myself. She wrote out, in wrenching detail, every episode in the last eight years when I had gone to a hospital, or blacked out, or missed work, or missed moments of my own children's lives. It was the first time someone had laid it out for me to see, every awful episode in its entirety, and it left me shaken. We took turns reading aloud from the book of Alcoholics Anonymous, full of stories of other people who had fallen hopelessly at the feet of this disease, only to find redemption.

Over and over, she hammered it home: "You cannot safely drink. Every attempt at controlled drinking ends disastrously. Your very life is at stake." Time and time again, she would pull out that timeline and point to it. "Do you see how powerless you are over alcohol? Where did your best thinking get you?" There was no denying my life had become unmanageable. It was right in front of me, in black and white.

But most important, Polly talked a lot about God. I am Catholic, and my parents are devout in their faith. I have always considered religion to be a personal matter, and I was frankly embarrassed when Polly started talking about prayer, and God, and how we have to turn it all over and ask for His guidance. She was unshakeable in her devotion to God. If she was aware of my discomfort, it didn't matter to her: her faith was that strong. Maybe she just knew I had to find my way to embracing it. I had spent my life praying in times of crisis. I wasn't an atheist convert in the foxhole, but I didn't pray regularly, and I sure didn't pray when times were good. Polly set out to show me a different way—and it has become a cornerstone in my recovery. When I was tearful about meeting with Marc to negotiate our divorce, she would say serenely, "Hand it over to God. He will guide you." When I had to go to ABC to meet with the president of the news division and persuade him to give me one last chance, she nodded and closed her eyes. "Pray. God will show you what to do."

Today, when I feel anxiety start to overtake me, I pray. When I feel angry, or resentful, or just cranky, I list every thing in my life that is a gift. And now I pray when times are good. I end each day by making a gratitude list—all the things I am grateful for that night. They can be big things like a long trip that went smoothly, or an interview I conducted at work that went really well. They can be small things, like a moment of laughter with my son, or just the way the sun sparkled on the river that evening, like a million shards of glass. And every single day, I thank God for my family, my health, my home, and a job that I still love.

I went back to work in November, fully aware there would not be another chance. I could not get back all the opportunities I had squandered, and I needed to stop looking with regret and shame over my own shoulder. I could only look forward and do my very best, every single day.

My recovery this time was different because I was not in a bubble at rehab; I was not in an alternate universe. I was home, confronted every hour of every day with what I had done. I could look into my sons' faces and see how I had hurt them. There was no escaping it; there was no denying it. The full extent of my disease and what I had done while in the throes of it was front and center in my life. I could not run away from it, as I had run away from every uncomfortable, anxious moment in my life. I had to navigate all the consequences of my drinking—the painful divorce, the two months off work, the incredulous glances I seemed to see everywhere from people who had read the news or heard the gossip. "She relapsed yet again? Can't she get it together?"

I took a class in Transcendental Meditation and learned

how to stop twice a day, center myself, and meditate. That and prayer have helped slow down the escalation of anxiety into panic, helped me not to take every single thing in life so personally. But these tools only work if you use them every single day, several times each day. They are not flimsy tools, as I had thought during that last summer and that terrible relapse. They are powerful weapons. They gave me the power to at last say no to drinking. The power to say yes to life.

Finally, I began once again going to meetings with other alcoholics, this time without my mantle of shame. I no longer hid in the back under a baseball cap. I sat up front. I listened to the stories I heard there, of other people's journeys and tragedies—the blackouts, the rehabs, the DUIs, the divorces, the children lost in custody battles, the livelihoods and the lives all lost to this disease. I listened to those stories with empathy and compassion, hoping someday I could learn to show myself those same qualities and gain some form of absolution. I heard their stories of redemption and victory, of how they now lived lives they never imagined possible—were happier than they ever dreamed—because they stopped drinking. And when it came time to share at the end of the meeting, I raised my hand and said out loud, "Hi, I'm Beth. I am an alcoholic."

—⚮—

Fall seven times. Stand up eight.

—JAPANESE PROVERB

No little girl lays awake in bed at night, dreaming of what she will become, and says fervently to herself, "I hope I grow up to be an alcoholic!" No wife and mother wakes up in the morning, stretches and yawns and says casually to herself, "This would be a good day to get so drunk I have to go to the emergency room." She doesn't pour breakfast cereal into a bowl and think, *Maybe I will even flirt with death and drink so much my blood alcohol level will be lethal.*

There are a lot of people who think alcoholism is a character defect, a weakness or a lack of self-discipline. I know, because I was one of them, even when I was deep into the disease. I kept thinking, *I will just cut back.* Later, I would berate myself: *For God's sake, get it together.* I was so disciplined in so many areas of my life—my work, my exercise, my diet, my budget. But all that focus and effort and willpower were useless for me when it came to alcohol. Because it truly is a disease, as the American

Medical Association said way back in 1966. Perhaps it is because we hurt so many others, as well as ourselves, when we drink. We do so much damage. Our loved ones and those near us recoil, or worse, bail altogether. Sometimes, we deserve that. But I can tell you that nearly every addict I know drank or took drugs because there was something else bigger that felt wrong, that hurt so much, it was unbearable. Numbing that "something else" became the only way to survive. We were, many of us, tormented souls who needed to find our way, however possible, to a place of grace.

Alcoholism and addiction have touched millions of people in this country. If you don't suffer from it, you know someone who does. We are your wives, your mothers, your daughters, your sisters. We are your children, your colleagues, your employees, your friends. We are Emmy award–winning journalists, Grammy award–winning singers, and Oscar-winning actors. We are diplomats and doormen, presidents and accountants, housewives and handymen. In the face of this disease we are all equal, the playing field leveled. If we are truly fortunate, we have employers who did not abandon us, family who stood by us, and perhaps someone who helped us find our way back, who never forgot that beneath all the appalling behavior there was a human being.

I am so very lucky for my family and my friends who stood by me. For years, my parents and my brother and sister were sick with worry... terrified that one day a call would come that I was dead. My family spent countless hours on the phone together, trying to figure out how to help me. My friend and producer Terri Lichstein was on many of those calls—and at my side during some of the worst times. I am deeply grateful to Ben Sherwood, James Goldston, Barbara Fedida, and David Sloan for giving me another chance at ABC News, for allowing me to return to the work I love. I am so fortunate that the producers and staff at *20/20* forgave me, and worked with me this past year. I am grateful Marc took such good care of our children during the times I could not, and that he tried his best to take care of me. I am thankful that he and I have found a way to be good parents to our boys together, even if we are now apart.

I wrote this book because when I first worried I had a drinking problem, I read other peoples' books about their battles with the disease—mostly women. I spent my whole life looking at other people and thinking their lives were perfect and easy and wonderful, while mine was not. Maybe someone watching me on television, or seeing me in an airport, or walking down the street, thought the same thing about me. Perhaps my story will show them everyone has something they struggle with, something difficult and painful. There is a saying in recovery that you are only as sick as your secrets. Now my secrets are out. Part of me is absolutely terrified. I know some people have already heard a different narrative about the blackout, the visits to the emergency rooms, the drunken vacations, the trips to rehab. I have lived in fear that those stories would leak out to the press, as tiny bits of it already have. Now the narrative is mine. I must own my story, and I must take responsibility for my role in the end of my marriage. I still feel enormous guilt and anguish over what I did, and the people I hurt. I will never get back all the precious moments I lost with my sons, and that is perhaps the most bitter pill of all. I remind myself every day that I cannot undo what I have done, that I need to focus on what I can do now and be the best mother possible to these two incredible boys I am so lucky to have. They tell me they have forgiven me for what I did while drinking. I pray someday I will find the power to forgive myself.

Today, am I cured of alcoholism? No, one is never cured. It is a daily battle, a daily choice. I have heard alcoholics with twenty-four years of sobriety say, "Thank God I am sober today," and mean it. They have learned and embraced a valuable lesson. Today is all we have. That's all anyone has, really. When I walk down the street, past restaurants and wine bars, I still sometimes glance at the tables of people enjoying what I cannot. I take in their glasses, half filled, and their easy camaraderie, and I feel envious. I still sometimes pass a liquor store and shudder with memories of my secret trips there to stock up. But that happens less and less now. Even more surprising to me is that my anxiety—my lifelong nemesis—has waned. Somewhere in my journey, the alcohol that I used to calm myself turned into kerosene—igniting small blazes of worry into bonfires of panic. It is still amazing to me how manageable my anxiety is, now that I am not drinking.

Every day I make the choice not to drink, the choice to be present in every moment, even the difficult ones. And every night I thank God for another day of sobriety. I do not take it for granted. Not now, when I have seen how quickly everything good about my life can dissolve in a glass of wine, never to be recovered. I am responsible for my own sobriety, and my own happiness. I cannot expect other people to fix my problems, or blame them when things go wrong. Learning that lesson has helped me take ownership of my own life again. It's not perfect, it's sometimes really hard. But it's mine, and it's up to me to make the most of it, and there is so much to be so thankful for.

I think back often to that hike I took up that mountain in Utah on my last day at Cirque. How I thought so many times that it was too hard, that the journey to the top was too far. I remember how I looked around at the beauty all around me and decided then to soldier on, timing my breath to my steps. Slow and steady, breathing in, breathing out. And between breaths, never forgetting the lesson I learned that day about recovery, about life, a lesson I now remember every single day. One step at a time, one day at a time. Be strong. Be grateful. Just do the next right thing, and you will arrive.

—ɷ—

Acknowledgments

I would like to thank Peter Kaminsky for his help and expert guidance in this last year—I could not have written this book without him. My deepest thanks to my editor, Gretchen Young, and my agent, Cait Hoyt, for their endless patience and encouragement to be brave and honest in these pages. They never let me forget that I am not the only one in the world who has struggled with anxiety and addiction, and that there are others out there who might feel less alone by reading my story.

About the Author

ELIZABETH VARGAS is the co-anchor of *20/20* on ABC News. She resides in Manhattan with her two children.